Olaf Neubauer   Bookkeeping, Cost Accounting and Economics

Olaf Neubauer

unter Mitwirkung von

Antje Praefcke und Carol Otterbach

Bookkeeping, Cost Accounting and Economics

Introduction to Business Administration and Management

Copyright:

Alle Rechte für dieses Buch liegen beim Autor. Da das Werk einschließlich aller seiner Teile urheberrechtlich geschützt ist, darf kein Teil dieses Lehrbuchs in irgendeiner Form (durch Fotokopie, Mikrofilm oder ein anderes Verfahren) ohne schriftliche Genehmigung des Autors reproduziert oder unter Verwendung elektronischer Systeme verarbeitet, vervielfältigt oder verbreitet werden.

1. Auflage, Dezember 2006

Herstellung und Verlag: Books on Demand GmbH, Norderstedt

ISBN 3-8334-6921-8
ISBN 978-3-8334-6921-3

Vorwort

Dieses Lehrbuch ist aus jahrelanger Unterrichtspraxis entstanden und soll Studenten der Fachrichtung Wirtschaft, die beabsichtigen, ihr Studium im englischsprachigen Ausland fortzusetzen oder dort zu arbeiten, mit dem englischen Wirtschaftsvokabular vertraut machen, um ein zielgerichtetes und erfolgreiches Studieren und Arbeiten in diesen Ländern zu verwirklichen. Dasselbe gilt auch für Mitarbeiter von größeren Unternehmen aus dem deutschsprachigen Raum, die Kontakte zu Zweigstellen ihres Unternehmens oder Kunden im englischsprachigen Ausland haben. Ebenso können Erwachsene in der Weiterbildung, Schüler der Sekundarstufe II, besonders an Wirtschaftsgymnasien, und auch Schüler, die an Austauschprogrammen mit Schulen in englischsprachigen Ländern teilnehmen, von den in diesem Buch dargestellten Inhalten profitieren.

Infolge eines steigenden internationalen Wettbewerbs und einer zunehmenden Globalisierung, die nicht ohne Auswirkungen auf die zukünftigen Arbeitsplatzanforderungen und die individuelle Handlungskompetenz sind, kommen den neuen Informations- und Kommunikationstechnologien, aber auch den Schlüsselqualifikationen, wie z. B. Denken in Zusammenhängen, Problemlöse-, Kommunikations- und Entscheidungsfähigkeit, Selbstständigkeit, Teamarbeit, Flexibilität sowie dem lebenslangen Lernen eine immer größer werdende Bedeutung zu. Daher ist es besonders wichtig, über gute Fremdsprachenkenntnisse zu verfügen, wobei die englische Sprache, insbesondere das englische Fachvokabular, auf den unterschiedlichsten wissenschaftlichen Gebieten eine äußerst bedeutende Funktion einnimmt.

Um den Leser nicht mit praxisfernen Sonderfällen zu überfluten, wurden in allen Kapiteln nur die elementaren wirtschaftswissenschaftlichen Grundlagen aufgezeigt. Zudem wird ein bereits bestehendes Grundwissen über wirtschaftliche Zusammenhänge in deutscher Sprache vorausgesetzt. Spezialfälle sind in der umfangreichen englischsprachigen Wirtschaftsliteratur nachzulesen. Die sich dabei ergebenden fachspezifischen Vokabeln können z. B. kostenlos unter der Internetadresse www.leo.org nachgeschlagen werden.

Anhand der Arbeitsaufgaben am Ende jedes Kapitels kann man das Gelernte und selbst Erarbeitete überprüfen. Aufgrund der zahlreichen, problemorientierten Übungsaufgaben, die sowohl in Einzel- als auch in Gruppenarbeit unter Berücksichtigung des handlungsorientierten Lernansatzes bearbeitet werden können, eignet sich dieses Lehrbuch zum Selbststudium, zum Einsatz an Universitäten, Akademien und Wirtschaftsgymnasien und überdies in Kursen bei privaten Bildungsträgern.

Das vorliegende Buch hätte ohne die stets engagierte Mitarbeit von Frau Antje Praefcke, Wirtschaftsexpertin bei der Commerzbank in Frankfurt/Main und internationale Währungsanalystin in Rundfunk und Fernsehen, sowie Frau Carol Otterbach, Dozentin am Seminar für Anglistik an der TU Braunschweig, nicht erscheinen können. Beiden danke ich sehr für die von ihnen übernommenen Lektorats- und Korrekturarbeiten und zugleich für die inhaltlichen und methodischen Anregungen aus der Sicht ihrer Berufspraxis.

Besonderer Dank gilt Herrn Oberstudiendirektor Dr. Ulrich Kühnast, Schulleiter der Ludwig-Erhard-Schule in Salzgitter-Lebenstedt, der mich bereits während meiner Schulzeit zu meinem späteren Studium der Wirtschaftspädagogik inspirierte. An der von ihm geleiteten Schule absolvierte ich mein Referendariat und bin dort wieder seit dem Jahr 2004 tätig.

Braunschweig, im Oktober 2006
Olaf Neubauer
Studienrat an der
Ludwig-Erhard-Schule,
Salzgitter-Lebenstedt

Contents

1 Bookkeeping — 10
1.1 The Balance Sheet — 10
1.2 Different Balance Sheet Changes — 16
1.3 Revenues and Expenses — 20
1.4 Inventory and Different Methods of its Valuation for the Calculation of the Cost of Sales — 23
1.5 Depreciation Methods for Noncurrent Assets — 27
1.6 Equity and Liabilities — 31
1.7 What is a Cash Flow Statement? — 35
1.8 Ratios — 42

2 Cost Accounting — 51
2.1 Introduction — 51
2.2 Cost Element Accounting — 52
2.3 Cost Center Accounting — 55
2.3.1 What is Cost Center Accounting? — 55
2.3.2 Cost Allocation Methods — 56
2.3.2.1 Direct Allocation Method — 57
2.3.2.2 Step-Down Allocation Method — 59
2.3.2.3 Reciprocal Allocation Method — 61
2.4 Product Cost Accounting — 65
2.4.1 Product Costing Scheme — 65
2.4.2 Products of a Joint Production Process — 66
2.4.3 Accounting for By-Products — 70
2.4.4 Product Costing per Period — 72
2.5 Cost-Volume-Profit (CVP) Analysis — 74
2.5.1 Essentials of CVP Analysis — 74
2.5.2 Mathematical Methods for Determining the Break-even Point — 76
2.5.2.1 Equation Method — 77
2.5.2.2 Contribution Margin Method — 77
2.5.2.3 Graph Methods — 78
2.5.2.3.1 Cost-Volume-Profit Graph — 78
2.5.2.3.2 Profit-Volume Graph — 79

2.6	What is the Difference between Variable Costing and Absorption Costing?	82
2.6.1	Introduction	82
2.6.2	Calculating and Explaining Differences in Operating Income	83
2.6.3	Advantages and Disadvantages of Absorption Costing	90
2.6.4	Combination of Absorption and Variable Costing with Actual, Normal and Standard Costing	92
2.6.5	Different Denominator-Level Capacity Concepts for Absorption Costing	93
2.6.6	Stepwise Contribution Accounting	95
3	**Economics**	**99**
3.1	Vocational School, Apprenticeship and Banking	99
3.2	Quantitative Models for the Planning, Management and Control of Stocks	105
3.2.1	Introduction	105
3.2.2	Economic Order Quantity	106
3.2.2.1	Tabulation Method	108
3.2.2.2	Graphical Method	108
3.2.2.3	Formula Method	109
3.2.3	Economic Order Quantity with Respect to Quantity Discount	111
3.2.4	Determining the Re-order Point and other Stock Figures	112
3.2.5	ABC Classification Method	114
3.3	Benchmarking	118
3.4	Office Equipment	118
3.5	Capital Investment Decisions	120
3.5.1	Discounted Cash Flow (DCF) Methods	120
3.5.1.1	Net Present Value (NPV) Method	121
3.5.1.2	Internal Rate of Return (IRR) Method	123
3.5.1.3	Comparison of NPV and IRR Method	125
3.5.1.4	Modified Internal Rate of Return (MIRR) Method	127
3.5.2	Methods Ignoring the Time Value of Money	129
3.5.2.1	Payback Method	129
3.5.2.2	Accounting Rate of Return Method	131

Appendix 135
Table 1: Discount Factors 135
Table 2: Cumulative Discount Factors 135

Chronological Vocabulary List 136

Alphabetical Vocabulary List (English – German) 158

Alphabetical Vocabulary List (German – English) 180

Chapter 1: Bookkeeping

1.1 The Balance Sheet

Every balance sheet gives information about an entity at one point in time. An entity is any organization or business. The balance sheet shows the financial position of an entity as of one moment in time, in general as of December 31. Balance sheets are structured according to increasing liquidation in Germany, whereas in the USA the amounts on a balance sheet are always listed with the most current items first. Every balance sheet has two sides: the assets are found on the left, the equity and liabilities on the right side. A total is always given for each side of a balance sheet.

Assets are <u>valuable resources</u>, they have been acquired at a <u>measurable cost</u>, are <u>owned by an entity</u> and are required in order to operate. Liabilities are obligations of the entity to creditors who have a claim against the company. There are different sources of equity funds, e. g. paid-in capital and retained profits (= retained earnings). The note "000 omitted" means that every item of the balance sheet is reported in thousands of dollars, because the numbers are easier to read without the last three digits.

There are differences between the principles and regulations in German accounting law and US GAAP. In Germany financial statements have to be drawn up in accordance with GAAP (GoB, § 243 (1)), Commercial Code). Further principles of preparation for financial statements follow.
Financial statements have to be
- clear and understandable (§ 243 (2)),
- complete (§ 246 (1)),
- prepared in the German language and be expressed in Euro (§ 244),

- signed by the businessman and dated. If there are several personally liable partners, then all are required to sign (§ 245).
- Offsetting is prohibited (§ 246 (2)) so that neither assets may be offset against liabilities nor income against expenses.

There are some further valuation provisions to the valuation of assets and liabilities in financial statements (§ 252 (1) - (6)) and § 253:

(1) Balance sheet continuity: the amounts which are included in the opening balance sheet must agree with those of the closing balance sheet of the preceding financial year.
(2) Going concern concept: the accounting and valuation principles normally assume a going concern to the extent.
(3) The assets and liabilities have to be valued at the balance sheet date on an item by item basis.
(4) Prudence concept: According to the imparity principle, all anticipated risks and losses which arise up to the balance sheet date have to be taken into account, even if they become known between the balance sheet date and the date on which the financial statements are prepared. According to the realisation principle, profits may only be taken up if they are realised at the balance sheet date.
(5) Accruals concept / matching principle: Income and expenses of the financial year have to be taken up in the financial statements, regardless of the point in time of the related payments.
(6) Consistency concept: the valuation methods of preceding financial statements should be retained.
(7) Historical cost principle: Assets are not stated at more than their purchase or manufacturing cost, reduced by their depreciation; liabilities are to be stated at their redemption amount.

The legal representatives of a corporation have to prepare financial statements, consisting of a balance sheet, a profit and loss account and notes to the financial statements. The financial statements of a corporation must, in compliance with generally accepted accounting principles, present a true and fair view of the net worth, financial position and results of the company (§ 264 (2)). The notes contain explanatory comments as prescribed for the individual headings of the balance sheet and the profit and loss account, but the external form, structure and extent of the notes are not covered by specific provisions.

The management report, which contains no detailed information, is not a part of the financial statements but is required for the annual report of a corporation. The management report should contain as a minimum a description of the development of the business, post balance sheet date events of special importance, the situation and development of the corporation and its area of research and development.

The contents and extent of financial statements are derived from specific rules of the laws and ordinances and from the Third Book of the Commercial Code, whereby the form of presentation and the extent of the information required allow differences according to legal form, size and industry. In order to simplify the preparation, audit and disclosure of financial statements, size classifications of corporations were introduced (§ 267):

Size Classes of Corporations	Balance Sheet Totals (Million Euros)	Sales Volume (Million Euros)	Number of Employees
Large	> 13,75	> 27,5	> 250
Medium-Sized	> 3,438 <= 13,75	> 6,875 <= 27,5	51 <= 250
Small	<= 3,438	<= 6,875	<= 50

Small corporations are those which do not exceed at least two of the three criteria for small corporations. Medium-sized corporations are those which exceed at least two of the three criteria for small corporations but do not exceed at least two of the three criteria for medium sized corporations. Large corporations are those which exceed at least two of the three criteria for medium-sized corporations. The average number of employees is the fourth part of the sum of the numbers employed at March 31, June 30, September 30 and December 31, including those employed abroad but excluding trainees.

Current assets are expected to be converted into cash or used up in the near future, normally within one year. Inventories, accounts receivable, securities, checks, cash on hand and cash in banks belong to the current assets. Prepaid expenses are intangible assets disclosing payments prior to the balance sheet date which represent expenditure for a definite period after this date.

Fixed assets are expected to be useful for longer than one year. Trademarks, patents and goodwill are intangible assets, which belong to the fixed assets. Goodwill arises when a company buys another enterprise and pays more than the value of its net assets. Goodwill is not an asset unless it is purchased. Land, buildings, machines and other equipment are tangible assets which also belong to the fixed assets. The accumulated depreciation must be subtracted from the original cost of fixed assets if they have been used up.

Current liabilities are claims that become due within a short time, normally one year. Long-term liabilities normally become due after more than one year. Accruals for pensions and estimated tax accruals are accrued liabilities (= accruals). They have to be set up for uncertain liabilities and for anticipated losses from uncompleted transactions. Deferred income are liabilities disclosing receipts prior to the balance sheet date which represent income of a specific period after that date.

Subscribed capital, capital reserves (= paid-in capital), earnings reserves, retained earnings or accumulated losses brought forward and net income or net loss for the year belong to the equity. Retained earnings are additions to equity of a company that have accumulated since the entity began; they are not of a single year and show the amount of capital generated by operating activities that has been retained in the entity after dividends have been paid.

Questions and Tasks

1. Which of the following items belong to the asset of a company in accounting?
   a. the employees,
   b. a building rented by a company,
   c. a building owned by a company,
   d. the reputation of a company,
   e. the value of the trademark of a company, developed through its own efforts,
   f. a trademark of a company, if this company was purchased by another company, including an item called "trademarks, patents and goodwill" valued at some million dollars,
   g. an old computer, purchased for $ 1,000 ten years ago, but now worthless,
   h. clothes that nobody wants to buy because they are out of style.
   i. List further items which do not belong to the asset of a company in accounting.

2. How much is the equity of this company?
   total assets: $ 240,000,
   total liabilities: $ 200,000.

3. Which of the following facts could be stated in a balance sheet of a company?
   a. the fitness of the staff,
   b. the number of cars,
   c. the amount of cash.
   d. List further facts of a company that cannot be stated in a balance sheet.

4. A department store purchased goods for $ 9,000. The owners think that they can sell these goods to customers for $ 12,000. At what amount should these goods be reported on the balance sheet of the department store?

5. Prepare a balance sheet (000 omitted), using the following items correctly listed and translating them into English:

Gebäude	800	kurzfr. Verbindlichk.	300
Bank	50	Waren	450
Maschinen	150	langfr. Verbindlichk.	200
Forderungen	75	Ladenausstattung	50
Kasse	25	Eigenkapital	?
Anlagevermögen	?	Umlaufvermögen	?

How much are the equity and the current ratio?

6. To which size classification do the following corporations belong?

Name of the Corporation	Balance Sheet Totals (Million Euros)	Sales Volume (Million Euros)	Number of Employees	Size Class of Corporation
Blue Company	8	30	60	
White Company	3	7	40	
Gold Company	14	27	270	
Green Company	12	30	44	
Red Company	25	40	30	

1.2 Different Balance Sheet Changes

A transaction is an event that is recorded in the accounting records and causes at least two changes on the balance sheet, not counting a possible change in the totals. Therefore accounting is called a double-entry-system.

Instead of changing balance sheet amounts directly, accounts are used to record each change. Each account resembles a large T, so it is called a T-account. The title of each account is written on the top of each T. The currency of the different amounts is not named in each account.

Asset accounts are on the left side of a balance sheet (both opening balance sheet and closing balance sheet), the beginning balance (= opening balance) is recorded on the left side of the T-account. In any asset account, an increase must always be recorded on the left side and a decrease on the right side.

Liability and equity accounts are on the right side of a balance sheet, the beginning balance is recorded on the right side of the T-account. In these accounts, an increase must always be recorded on the right side and a decrease on the left side.

In all T-accounts increases are added to the beginning balance at the end of each accounting period and the total of the decreases is subtracted from it. The result is called the new balance.

The left side of a T-account is called the debit side, the right side is the credit side. Increases in asset accounts and decreases in liability and equity accounts are recorded on the debit side (= to debit an account), decreases in asset accounts and increases in liability and equity accounts are recorded on the credit side (= to credit an account). The word debit is abbreviated as "Dr.", the word credit as "Cr.".

The total of all debit balances always equals the total of all credit balances.

(debit or Dr.)	Asset account	(credit or Cr.)
beginning balance		decreases
Increases		

(debit or Dr.)	Liability or Equity account	(credit or Cr.)
Decreases		beginning balance
		increases

The amount by which equity increased because of operations during a period of time (e. g. the sale of merchandise) is called the income of that period. The income statement or the profit and loss statement explains the income within a period of time.

The increase in retained earnings resulting from operations during a period of time is called a revenue, the decrease is called an expense. Increases in revenues, liabilities and equity are credits, increases in expenses are debits. The difference between revenues and expenses is the income, also called profit or earnings. When the closing entries are done, the balances in revenues and expenses are transferred to an account called Income Summary (= profit and loss account). Normally the revenues account has a credit balance, the expenses account has a debit balance. The profit and loss account is closed to the retained earnings account, because the income within a period is an increase in retained earnings and therefore an increase in equity.

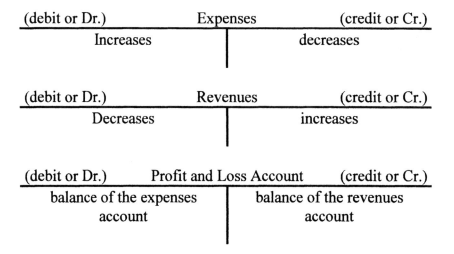

Retained earnings only refers to the amount of income that has been retained in the company since the entity began. Therefore, if there are any withdrawals out of the income for personal use, the retained earnings are reduced by the corresponding amount.

Before transactions are recorded in the ledger, they are written as they happen in a journal (= book of original). This record is called a journal entry (original entry, prime entry). The account which is debited is listed first, the account which is credited is listed below. The journal entries are transferred to the ledger, where several accounts can be found. This transaction is called posting or entering.

If merchandise costing 40 is sold for 50 and the customer agrees to pay within some days, this transaction is recorded in the journal as follows:

Dr.	Accounts Receivable	50	
	Cr. Revenues		50

Dr.	Expenses	40	
	Cr. Merchandise		40

Dr.	Revenues	50	
	Cr. Profit and Loss Account		50

Dr.	Profit and Loss Account	40	
	Cr. Expenses		40

Dr.	Profit and Loss Account	10	
	Cr. Retained Earnings		10

Questions and Tasks

1. Beginning balance (000 omitted):

Buildings	460	Equity	?
Equipment	80	Current liabilities	64
Merchandise	110	Long-term liabilities	360
Accounts receivable	43		
Cash on hand	10		
Cash in banks	62		

Complete the record of the following transactions in the accounts of a ledger sheet and do the closing entries:

a. The company borrowed 7 from a bank.
b. Merchandise costing 40 was purchased for cash.
c. Merchandise costing 60 was purchased on credit.
d. The company received 10 in cash from a credit customer.
e. The company paid 12 to a creditor.
f. Merchandise costing 60 was sold for 90. The customer agreed to pay the receipt within 30 days.

1.3 Revenues and Expenses

The income statement describes changes in equity during an accounting period. The fiscal year is normally the calendar year. Revenues cause increases in equity, whereas expenses cause decreases in equity. They both are not necessarily accompanied, at the same time, by increases or decreases in cash. Revenue which is recognized in the period in which services are **delivered** can be realized before (a.), during (b.) or after (c.) the period in which the cash from the sale is received. The journal entries for these transactions are:

a. Revenue before cash receipt
Entry for the sale on credit:
Dr.   Accounts Receivable
    Cr.   Sales Revenue

Entry when the customer pays for the credit purchase:
Dr.   Cash
    Cr.   Accounts Receivable

b. Revenue at the time of cash receipt
Dr.   Cash
    Cr.   Sales Revenue

c. Revenue after cash receipt
Entry for the payment in advance:
Dr.   Cash
    Cr.   Advances from Customers

Entry when the merchandise is delivered:
Dr.   Advances from Customers
    Cr.   Sales Revenue

The account advances from customers is listed on the right side of the balance sheet, because the obligation to deliver a product which a customer has paid for in advance is a liability for the supplier.

There are different types of revenues, such as sales revenue, rental revenue and interest revenue.

If a customer does not pay the goods delivered, the supplier has a bad debt and cannot realize revenue from this transaction so that his equity decreases. For such expenses the accountants use a separate account to write off the bad debt, called allowance for doubtful accounts, in order to decrease the accounts receivable and the sales revenue of the supplier.

The purchase of goods or services is an expenditure which results in a decrease in an asset, e. g. cash, or an increase in liabilities without any changes in equity. When some of these goods are used up or consumed in the operations of the business, an expense results since assets and equity decrease. When products are sold and delivered, their costs are matched with revenues in this period, so that their costs become expenses.

There are different types of expenses, such as prepaid expenses (for intangible assets that will become expenses in future periods), insurance expense, depreciation expense for tangible assets, salary expense, pension expense, rent expense and losses due to destruction, fire, theft or other reasons if they are reasonably possible. Liabilities for expenses incurred but not paid up to the present are called accrued liabilities, such as accrued salaries, accrued pensions or accrued rent.

There are two sources of equity:

a. paid-in capital, which is the capital supplied by investors and
b. retained earnings, i. e. earnings resulting from profitable operations retained in the company.

There is no standard format for an income statement, but normally the first item is sales revenue which describes the amount of products delivered to customers during a period of time. The following expenses are subtracted from this item:

- cost of sales (cost of goods of which the revenue is reported by the first item),
- operating expenses (costs related to the current period and costs that do not benefit future profits);
- provision for income taxes.

The result is called net income or net loss. Dividends, which are a distribution of earnings to shareholders but not an expense, must be subtracted from net income before this amount can be added to retained earnings at the beginning of the fiscal year in order to determine retained earnings at the end of the accounting period.

Questions and Tasks

1. Geb Kunath Company manufactures a chair and places it in its retail store in January. Harry Farmer, a customer, agrees to buy this chair in February. The chair is delivered to him in March, and he pays the invoice in April. When is the revenue recognized?

2. Jürgen Neubauer Company agrees to sell a computer to Fabian Bosse, a customer, for $ 1,800, in September, and the customer makes a down payment of $ 300 at that time. The cost of the computer was $ 1,200. The computer is

delivered to Fabian Bosse in October, but the customer pays the remaining $ 1,500 in November.

Do the journal entries that would be made in September, October and November for both the revenue and expense aspects of this transaction. Label each entry with the proper month.

3. What is the difference between an expenditure and an expense?

4. Describe the term net income.

1.4 Inventory and Different Methods of its Valuation for the Calculation of the Cost of Sales

"Cost of sales" and "cost of goods sold" still mean the same. If a dealer sells goods at a value of $ 3,000 for $ 4,000, these transactions have to be recorded in the journal as the following entries:

Dr.	Cash	4,000	
	Cr. Sales Revenues		4,000 and

Dr.	Cost of Sales	3,000	
	Cr. Inventory		3,000

At the end of each accounting period, companies which do not take a perpetual inventory count their goods. This process is called taking a physical inventory, by which each item is reported at its cost and not at its selling price. If goods are stolen, damaged or spoiled, there will be negative effects on the equity because of this shrinkage.

Cost of sales are calculated as follows:

    beginning inventory
+ purchases
= total goods available
- ending inventory
= cost of sales

Most companies enter the inventory at different unit costs during the accounting period, so that it is difficult to assign the ending inventory. There are three different methods for calculating the ending inventory and the cost of sales:

a. First-In, First-Out Method (FIFO)
The assumption is that the goods that came into the inventory first are the first to move out, so that the older units were sold during the accounting period and the newer remain in the ending inventory.

b. Last-In, First-Out Method (LIFO)
The LIFO method assumes that the newest units (last units purchased) were the first to be sold during the accounting period and the older remain in the inventory.

c. Average Cost Method
The ending inventory and the cost of sales during an accounting period are calculated at the average cost per unit of the goods available.

In periods of rising prices the cost of sales is higher under LIFO than under FIFO. Therefore, the taxable income and income tax are lower under LIFO than under FIFO if prices are rising. In this case the LIFO method is preferred by most companies. Companies cannot switch back and forth between these three methods of calculating the ending inventory and the cost of sales. In several countries the LIFO method is not permitted.

If the market value of an item of inventory at the end of an accounting period is lower than its original cost, the item has to be "written down" to its market value, so that the inventory account is credited and cost of sales is debited.

In a manufacturing company the production cost consists of three elements: **direct materials, direct labor and overheads,**
which are added together in order to determine the total cost of the finished products. Until the products are sold, their costs are held in inventory, when they are sold, this amount becomes cost of sales.

Costs are divided in two categories:

a. product costs: these are associated with the production of goods, e. g. direct materials, direct labor and production overhead costs. The product costs of goods become cost of sales in the period in which the goods are sold, which can be later than the period in which these products were manufactured.

b. period costs: these are associated with the sales and general activities of the company during the accounting period, e. g. some overhead costs such as the cost of heating the offices of the sales department. These costs are treated as operating expenses of the period in which they are incurred.

Questions and Tasks

1. A retailer sells a TV that had cost $ 1,600 for $ 2,000. Write the journal entries for the four accounts which are affected by this transaction.

2. Calculate the cost of sales for the accounting period and inventory at the end of the accounting period by the FIFO, LIFO and average cost methods:

	Quantity of Units	Unit Cost	Total Cost
Inventory, January 1	800	$ 1.00	
Purchase, March 4	500	$ 1.10	
Purchase, June 2	700	$ 1.50	
Ending inventory, December 31	400		

Method of Inventory Valuation	Cost of Sales	Inventory, December 31
FIFO		
LIFO		
Average Cost		

3. A company finds out that the market value of its inventory is $ 9,000 lower than its cost. Write the journal entries.

4. In what period do
   a. product costs become an expense
   b. period costs become an expense?

1.5 Depreciation Methods for Noncurrent Assets

When a tangible noncurrent asset is acquired, it is recorded in the accounts at its cost, including all costs incurred to make it available for its use, e. g. purchase price, fees, transportation and installation costs.

A capital lease is a long-term lease so that the lessee controls this fixed asset for almost its whole life and can record the leased item as an asset although it is owned by the lessor.

Land is reported on the balance sheet at its acquisition cost even if the market value rises but not if the market value is lower than the acquisition costs. Plant assets, however, have a limited service life (= useful life) which cannot be known exactly when they are acquired.

Depreciation involves treating a portion of the cost of a plant asset as an expense, called depreciation expense, during each year of its estimated service life until finally it is used up. There are several reasons for depreciation of a fixed asset, e. g.: when it wears out or becomes obsolete. The amount that a company expects to sell a plant asset for at the end of its service life is called its residual value. The depreciable cost of a plant asset is calculated by subtracting its residual value from its total cost.

There are several depreciation methods for the calculation of the depreciation expense in each year of the estimated service life of a plant asset:

a. Unit-of-Production Depreciation Method
In this depreciation method, a cost per unit of production is calculated. The depreciation expense for each year of the service life of the plant asset is

found by multiplying the unit cost by the number of units that the fixed asset produced during that year.

b. Straight-Line Depreciation

The depreciation expense during each year of the estimated service life of a plant asset is an equal fraction of the depreciable cost of the asset. The percentage of the depreciation rate is calculated by the formula

(1 : number of the years of estimated service life of an asset) * 100.

The amount of depreciation expense each year is calculated by multiplying the depreciable cost by the depreciation rate.

c. Accelerated Depreciation

In this depreciation method, more depreciation expense is reported in the first years of the plant asset's service life in order to reduce the taxable income. In the later years of the fixed asset's service life, less depreciation expense is reported.

In accounting for depreciation the journal entries are

Dr. Depreciation expense
    Cr. Accumulated depreciation

Dr. Accumulated depreciation
    Cr. Plant

Accountants always prefer to show the original cost of each plant asset on the balance sheet each year. On the balance sheet, the balance in the accumulated depreciation account is deducted from the original cost of the plant asset, the remaining amount is the book value. When the cost of a plant asset has been completely written off as depreciaition expense, no more depreciation is recorded, even if the fixed asset is used furthermore, so that its depreciation expense from this point of time is zero.

If a plant asset is sold, the company can make a gain on sale or a loss on sale because of the difference between book value and the amount actually realized from the sale. The journal entries would be for an asset that had cost $ 20,000, had accumulated depreciation of $ 15,000 and was sold for $ 6,000:

Dr.	Cash	6,000	
Dr.	Accumulated depreciation	15,000	
	Cr. Plant		20,000
	Cr. Gain on sale of plant		1,000

The Internal Revenue Service (IRS) publishes regulations for calculating the taxable income. Sometimes there are differences between the tax accounting principles and the financial accounting principles, so that the taxable income differs from the financial accounting income. The difference between actual income tax paid to the government by the company and their income tax expense is called deferred income tax.

When the supply of wasting assets, i. e. natural resources such as natural gas, coal, oil, minerals or timber, is reduced, the depletion is also reported on the balance sheet, but the asset account is reduced directly so that an accumulated depletion account is not used. The asset is depleted by multiplying the quantity of the resource used in a period by its unit cost.

Amortization means writing off the cost of intangible assets, e. g. patents, but only if they have been acquired at a measurable cost.

Questions and Tasks

1. A machine is acquired at a cost of $ 11,000. Its expected service life is 5 years and its estimated residual value is $ 1,000.

   a. How much is the depreciable cost of the machine?

   b. How much is the depreciation rate for this machine, if the straight line depreciation is used?

   c. What amount will be recorded in the depreciation expense account of a ledger in each year of the asset's life?

   d. Complete the following table:

At the End of Year	Straight-Line Depreciation per Year	Book Value of the Machine
1		
2		
3		
4		
5		
Total		------------------

   e. What is the journal entry to record this depreciation expense?

2. A machine is acquired for $ 25,000. Its expected service life is 10 years and there is no residual value. Eleven years after the purchase of the machine, it is sold for $ 1,500 in cash.

   What is the journal entry to record this?

3. A company purchased a truck for $ 22,000. The manager expects that the truck would provide services for 100,000 miles and would have a residual value of $ 2,000.

   a. How much is the depreciable cost of the truck?

b. How much is the estimated cost per mile?

c. How much is the depreciation expense, if the truck was driven 70,000 miles in a year?

4. A company purchased a coal mine for $ 2,400,000 and expected that it would contain 120,000 tons of coal.

a. How much is the unit cost per ton?

b. How much is the depletion expense, if the company mined 30,000 tons of coal?

c. How much will the coal mine asset be reported on the balance sheet after the company mined 30,000 tons of coal?

1.6 Equity and Liabilities

There are two sources of equity capital: paid-in-capital and retained earnings. The equity item in a sole proprietorship is often reported without listing its two sources separately but by giving the sole proprietor's (= sole trader's) name, followed by the word capital. If there are only a few partners in a partnership (general partnership or limited partnership), the equity of each (both general and limited partner) might be shown separately, by giving the partner's name, followed also by the word capital.

Corporations like public limited companies issue shares (= stocks) in order to increase the shareholder's equity: the common shareholders (= stockholders) hold common stocks, the preferred shareholders hold preferred stocks that give its owners preferential treatment over the common sharholders. Shares bought back by the issuing company are called treasury shares (= treasury stock).

A public limited company need not repay the amount the shareholders have invested. Furthermore, the shareholders can get a dividend, but the company is not obliged to pay a dividend. The retained earnings account decreases by the amount of dividends paid cash to shareholders. The journal entry for recording a dividend paid cash is

Dr. Retained Earnings
    Cr. Cash

A stock dividend consists of shares of stock in the corporation. Additional shares are issued in proportion to the number of shares that each shareholder owns, so that both the percentage of the total equity owned by each stockholder and the total amount of equity still stay the same.

Current assets are expected to be turned into cash within one year, current liabilities are obligations that become due within one year. The difference between current assets and current liabilites is called working capital.

The total of equity and noncurrent liabilities, which are also called debt capital, is called permanent capital.

A common source of debt capital is the issuance of bonds, which are a written promise to pay someone who lends money to a company. As time passes and the due date becomes less than one year, the bond becomes a current liability. The issuer is obligated to repay the principal and interest. Zero-coupon bonds do not pay interest, but the buyer purchases them for less than the principal amount and the issuer promises to pay the principal amount on the due date.

From the viewpiont of the issuing company, shares are a more expensive source of capital than bonds because investors expect a higher return from an investment in shares than from an investment in bonds. The former source of capital has a lower risk to the issuer than the latter because shares are not an obligation of the company that issues them, only bonds are an obligation.

A corporation which owns more than 50% of one or more other companies is called the parent company, and its controlled companies are called the subsidiaries. Each company has its own annual financial statements, the set for the whole family is called a set of consolidated financial statements. Intercompany transactions like purchase or sale between members of the family and the holding of shares of the subsidaries must be eliminated from the consolidated financial statements, from the consolidated profit and loss account (= consolidated income statement), from the consolidated retained earnings and from the consolidated balance sheet.

The consolidated profit and loss account reports revenues from all sales to outside parties only and all expenses resulting from costs incurred with outside parties. The consolidated balance sheet reports all the assets owned by the group and all the claims of parties outside the group. Only the individual balance sheets of the parent and its subsidiaries report the intercompany transactions.

Questions and Tasks

1. Miller Company
   Balance Sheet as of December 31, 20...

Assets		Liabilities	
Fixed Assets	40,000	Paid-in capital	14,000
Current Assets	20,000	Retained earnings	20,000
		Long-term liabilities	18,000
		Current liabilities	8,000
Total Assets	60,000	Total Equity and Liabilities	60,000

   a. How much is the working capital?

   b. How much is the permanent capital?

2. What are the differences between

   a. bonds and zero-coupon bonds?

   b. bonds and shares, that are both sources of permanent capital?

   c. a dividend paid in cash and a stock dividend?

3. Yellow Company owns 80 % of the stock of Green Company and 20 % of the stock of Blue Company.

   a. They had the following sales revenues: Yellow Company $ 2,000,000, Green Company $ 400,000 and Blue Company $ 800,000. Yellow Company sold $ 100,000 of products to Green Company and $ 50,000 of products to Blue Company, Green Company sold $ 25,000 of products to Blue Company.

      How much is the revenue reported on the consolidated income statement?

   b. Yellow Company has $ 100,000 cash, Green Company has $ 50,000 cash and Blue Company has $ 40,000 cash.

      How much is the item cash reported on the consolidated balance sheet?

1.7 What is a Cash Flow Statement?

An American company has to prepare three financial statements:
- the balance sheet in order to report the financial status of the company as of the end of each accounting period,
- the income statement, which focuses on profitability and reports the financial performance,
- the cash flow statement, which focuses on liquidity and reports the cash flow.

In contrast to German legislation, in the United States a cash flow statement has to be prepared by every company. There are a few small differences between the procedure of the IAS (= International Accounting Standards) and the US-GAAP (= Generell Accepted Accounting Principles).

The cash flow statement can be prepared by using the direct method, which summarizes the debits and credits to the cash account directly. The indirect method analyzes changes during the accounting period in the balance sheet items and analyzes the numbers on the income statement for the concerning accounting period. The result is the net increase or decrease in the cash account and cash equivalents (the difference between its ending balance and beginning balance).

Using the indirect method, the cash flow statement consists of three sections:
a. cash flow from operating activities,
b. cash flow from investing activities and
c. cash flow from financing activities.

a. Cash Flow from Operating Activities:

a₁. Changes in Current Assets, Current Liabilities and Working Capital

In order to find the amount of cash flow from operating activities, two adjustments to net income are made:

- for changes in working capital (current assets - current liabilities), excluding the item cash,
- for depreciaiton.

If the ending balance in a current asset (excluding cash), e. g. accounts receivable, is less than its beginning balance, the ultimate effect on cash is that the flow to cash is more than the amount of revenue, and an adjustment to net income is necessary in order to report this increase in cash.

If the ending balance in a current asset (excluding cash), e. g. accounts receivable, is greater than its beginning balance, the flow to cash is less than the amount of revenue, so that the net income amount has to be decreased in order to show the effect on cash.

Changes in current liabilities have the opposite effect on cash from changes in current assets, so that an increase in a current liability requires an adjustment to the net income amount in order to report this increase in cash. The result of a decrease in a current liability is that the net income amount has to be decreased because of the decrease in cash.

Finally, an increase in working capital results in a decrease in cash, and a decrease in working capital will result in an increase in cash.

Change	Adjustment to Net Income
Increase in a Current Asset	Decrease in Cash
Decrease in a Current Asset	Increase in Cash
Increase in a Current Liability	Increase in Cash
Decrease in a Current Liability	Decrease in Cash
Increase in Working Capital	Decrease in Cash
Decrease in Working Capital	Increase in Cash

a$_2$. Depreciation Expense

Depreciation expense is always subtracted from revenue in arriving at net income, but net income has to be adjusted by adding depreciation expense in order to find out the cash flow from operating activities.

b. Cash Flow from Investing Activities

If the ending balance in a noncurrent asset such as property, plant or equipment is greater than its beginning balance, e. g. because of purchase, this outflow of cash will result in a decrease of cash and has to be subtracted from net income.

If the ending balance in a noncurrent asset such as property, plant or equipment is less than its beginning balance, e. g. because of sale, this inflow of cash will result in an increase of cash and has to be added to net income.

c. Cash Flow from Financing Activities

The issuance and redemption of bonds, which are long-term and not current liabilities, or shares, which belong to shareholders' equity, and dividends paid are classified as financing activities.

If the ending balance in a noncurrent liability such as bonds is greater than its beginning balance, e. g. because of the issuance of bonds, this cash inflow must be added to net income. The issuance of additional shares of a company's stock also has to be added to net income.

If the ending balance in a noncurrent liability such as bonds is less than its beginning balance, e. g. because of the redemption of bonds, this cash outflow must be subtracted from net income. The redemption of shares of a company's stock and dividends paid also have to be subtracted from net income.

Summary of Cash Flow Statements

Cash flow statements are used to calculate an increase or a decrease in cash. The net increase in cash equals the difference between the ending balance and the beginning balance in cash. A forecast of cash flow helps managers, lenders and shareholders to estimate future needs for cash because of growth and investment or financial difficulties and to know about the ability to pay dividends and interest on debt and to repay the principal when it becomes due.

Statement of Cash Flow

Cash Flow from Operating Activities
   Net income
   + Decrease in non-cash current assets
   - Increase in non-cash current assets
   - Decrease in current liabilities
   + Increase in current liabilities
   + Depreciation expense
= Net cash flow from operating activities

Cash Flow from Investing Activities
   - Purchase of property, plant and equipment
   + Sale of property, plant and equipment
= Net cash flow from investing activities

Cash Flow from Financing Activities
   + Issuance of shares
   + Issuance of long-term borrowings (e. g. bonds)
   - Redemption of shares or bonds
   - Dividends paid
= Net cash flow from financing activities

   Net cash flow from operating activities
+ Net cash flow from investing activities
+ Net cash flow from financing activities
= Net increase or decrease in cash and cash equivalents
+ Cash and cash equivalents at beginning of period
= Cash and cash equivalents at end of period

Questions and Tasks

1. Adjust Blue Company's net income by using a cash flow statement in order to calculate the net increase in cash and cash equivalents and the ending balance in cash as of December 2002:

Blue Company
Balance Sheets (000 omitted)
As of December 31

	2002		2001	
Assets				
Current Assets				
Cash		?		17
Accounts receivable		50		52
Inventory		70		60
...				
Noncurrent assets				
Land		50		50
Plant, at cost	140		128	
Less accumulated depreciation	80	60	75	53
...				
Liabilities and Equity				
Current liabilities				
Accounts payable		40		42
Accrued wages		20		17
...				
Noncurrent liabilities				
Mortgage bonds payable		50		45
...				
Shareholder equity				
Paid-in capital		80		80
Retained earnings		96		81
...				

Black Company
Income Statement, 2002 (000 omitted)

Sales revenue	250
Less cost of sales	- 160
Gross margin	90
Less depreciaiton expense	- 5
...	
Net income	21
Less dividends	- 6
Addition to equity	15

2. Are the following transactions operating, investing or financing activities?

   a. Yellow Company buys an old truck for $ 100,000.

   b. Miller Corp. issues 5,000 shares of its common stock.

   c. Orange Company borrows $ 20,000 from City Bank, signing a short-term note payable.

   d. Give further examples for operating, investing and financing activities.

1.8 Ratios

There are several limitations in financial statements:
- they only report historical events that can be measured in monetary amounts,
- the market value of nonmonetary assets is not shown in a balance sheet,
- there are sometimes alternative ways of recording an event in an account, such as the LIFO, FIFO or average cost method,
- some accounting amounts are estimates, such as the service life and the residual value which are needed for calculating the depreciation expense of a plant assset.

An auditing is the examination of the accounting records by auditors, who are independent accountants and who write a report giving their evaluation of the company´s financial situation, which is reproduced in the company´s annual report.

Financial analysts form their evaluation of a company by calculating or studying the following ratios with all their different numerators and denominators. They also analyze the details of the financial statements and their notes and obtain additional information about the situation of a company by conversations and visits, since financial statements do not tell the whole story about a company.

a. Current Ratio

The current ratio is a measure of the ability of a company to pay its current obligations, which is also called liquidity. It is the ratio of current assets to current liabilities:

$$\text{Current ratio} = \frac{\text{Current assets}}{\text{Current liabilities}}$$

b. Days' Receivables

The ratio days' receivables describes the number of days of sales that are in accounts receivable at the end of the accounting period:

$$\text{Days' receivable} = \frac{\text{Accounts receivable} * 365}{\text{sales revenue}}$$

This ratio indicates if the customers of a company pay their bills when they are due.

c. Inventory Turnover Ratio

This ratio describes how many times the inventory turned over during an accounting period.

$$\text{Inventory turnover ratio} = \frac{\text{Cost of sales}}{\text{Inventory (at the end of the period)}}$$

If the inventory turnover is low, capital is tied up and the danger that the goods will become obsolete increases. If the inventory is too small, orders may not be filled promptly, so that customers will buy their goods at competitors. The turnover ratio will be increased
- if more goods are sold with the same level of inventory or
- if a company has less inventory for the same amount of sales volume.

d. Debt Ratio

This is the ratio of debt capital (= noncurrent liabilities) to total permanent capital. This ratio is a measure of the solvency of a company, which is the ability to pay its long-term obligations. Practically, most industrial companies have a debt ratio of less than 50%. Every company that obtains a high proportion of its permanent capital from debt is said to be highly leveraged.

$$\text{Debt ratio} = \frac{\text{Debt capital} * 100\%}{\text{Permanent capital}}$$

$$= \frac{\text{Debt capital} * 100\%}{\text{Debt capital} + \text{equity capital}}$$

$$= \frac{\text{Noncurrent liabilities} * 100\%}{\text{Noncurrent liabilities} + \text{equity}}$$

e. Return on Equity (ROE)

The percentage obtained by dividing net income by equity is called return on equity.

$$\text{Return on equity (ROE)} = \frac{\text{Net income} * 100\%}{\text{Equity}}$$

The return on equity in typical American corporations is about 15 %. The management and investors can compare the ROE of their company with its performance in earlier years (historical comparison) or with the ROE of other companies, especially when they are in the same industry as the own company (external comparison). On the contrary, the comparison of the amount of net income between two companies instead of their ratios does not provide useful information.

f. Gross Margin Percentage

Gross margin, calculated in the income statement of every company, is the difference between sales revenues and cost of sales. A high gross margin does not automatically lead to a high net income because of potential high expenses, which have to be subtracted from the gross margin in order to calculate the net income.

$$\text{Gross margin percentage} = \frac{\text{Gross margin} * 100\%}{\text{Sales revenue}}$$

$$= \frac{(\text{Sales revenue} - \text{cost of sales}) * 100\%}{\text{Sales revenue}}$$

g. Profit Margin Percentage

A further indication of profitability is the profit margin percentage, which is calculated by the following formula:

$$\text{Profit margin percentage} = \frac{\text{Net income} * 100\%}{\text{Sales revenue}}$$

h. Earnings per Share

This ratio is calculated by dividing the net income of a period by the numbers of shares outstanding.

$$\text{Earnings per share} = \frac{\text{Net income}}{\text{Number of shares outstanding}}$$

i. Price-Earnings-Ratio

This ratio is calculated by dividing the average market price of the stock by the earnings per share. If the average market price per share of a company was $ 40 and the earnings per share of this company was $ 5, the price-earnings ratio is 8 to 1.

$$\text{Price-earnings ratio} = \frac{\text{Average market price per share}}{\text{Earnings per share}}$$

j. Return on Permanent Capital, also called Return on Investment (ROI)

Both return on equity (ROE) and return on investment (ROI) are a measure of performance, taking into account both profitability and the capital used in generating profits. The ratio ROI is calculated by dividing Earnings Before the deduction of Interest and Taxes on income, abbreviated EBIT, instead of net income by permanent capital, which consists of equity and noncurrent liabilities:

$$\text{ROI} = \frac{EBIT * 100\%}{\text{Permanent capital}}$$

$$= \frac{EBIT * 100\%}{\text{Debt capital} + \text{equity}}$$

$$= \frac{EBIT * 100\%}{\text{Noncurrent liabilities} + \text{equity}}$$

k. EBIT margin

Here, EBIT is calculated as the percentage of sales revenue.

$$\text{EBIT margin} = \frac{EBIT * 100\%}{Sales\ revenue}$$

l. Capital Turnover

This ratio shows how much sales revenue was generated by permanent capital, so sales revenue is divided by permanent capital. In America, manufacturing companies have a capital turnover of about two times on average.

$$\text{Capital turnover} = \frac{Sales\ revenue}{Permanent\ capital}$$

$$= \frac{Sales\ revenue}{Debt\ capital + equity}$$

$$= \frac{Sales\ revenue}{Noncurrent\ liabilities + equity}$$

There is another way of calculating the return on investment by multiplying two other ratios:

$$\text{ROI} = \text{EBIT margin} * \text{Capital turnover}$$

$$= \frac{EBIT * 100\%}{Sales\ revenue} * \frac{Sales\ revenue}{Permanent\ capital}$$

$$= \frac{EBIT * 100\%}{Permanent\ capital}$$

Summary of some common ratios

No.	Ratio	Numerator	Denominator
1	Return on equity (ROE)	Net income * 100 (%)	Equity
2	Earnings per share	Net income	Number of shares outstanding
3	Price-earnings ratio	Average market price per share	Earnings per share
4	Return on permanent capital (= return on investment, ROI) (%)	EBIT * 100 (%)	Permanent capital (= Noncurrent liabilities + equity)
5	Gross margin (%)	Gross margin * 100 (%) (= Sales revenue - cost of sales) * 100 (%)	Sales revenue
6	Profit margin (%)	Net income * 100 (%)	Sales revenue
7	EBIT margin (%)	EBIT * 100 (%)	Sales revenue
8	Days' receivables	Accounts receivable * 365 (days)	Sales revenue
9	Inventory turnover (times)	Cost of sales	Inventory
10	Current ratio	Current assets	Current liabilities
11	Debt ratio	Debt capital * 100 (%) (= Noncurrent liabilities * 100 (%))	Permanent capital (= Noncurrent liabilities + equity)
12	Capital turnover	Sales revenue	Permanent capital (= Noncurrent liabilities + equity)

Questions and Tasks

1. A company has the following permanent capital:

Equity capital	$ 70,000
Debt capital	$ 30,000
Total	$ 100,000

   a. How much is the debt ratio of this company?

   b. Is this company highly leveraged?

2. The following financial statements are to be used in calculating the ratios of Black Company in 2001, listed in exercise a. to k.:

Black Company
Balance Sheet as of December, 2001 (000 omitted)

Assets
Current assets

Cash	30	Current liabilities	75
Accounts receivable	40	Noncurrent liabilities	100
Inventory	20	Shareholder equity	
Other	30	Paid-in capital	50
Total current assets	120	(4,000 shares outstanding)	
Noncurrent Assets	180	Retained earnings	75
		Total shareholder equity	125
Total assets	300	Total liabilities and equity	300

Black Company
Income Statement for 2001 (000 omitted)

Sales revenue	200
Cost of sales	120
Gross margin	80
Operating expenses	30
Earnings before interest and taxes	50
Interest and income taxes	30
Net income	20

How much was Black Company's

a. current ratio?

b. inventory turnover?

c. profit margin percentage?

d. debt ratio?

e. return on equity (ROE)?

f. EBIT margin?

g. capital turnover?

h. return on permanent capital (ROI)?

i. earnings per share?

j. price-earnings ratio if the average market price for each share during 2001 was $ 40?

k. gross margin percentage?

3. What is the difference between liquidity and solvency, and which are the ratios for measuring them?

Chapter 2: Cost Accounting

2.1 Introduction

Cost Accounting concentrates on the planning, control, variance and forecast of consumption resulting from internal business activities in order to determine the cost per unit, also called average cost, of products manufactured. Costs are the rated consumption of all goods and services for the production of output.

One must distinguish between fixed costs and variable costs. Fixed costs remain unchanged in total for a given time period despite wide changes in the related level of output and become progressively smaller per unit if production increases. Examples of fixed costs include depreciation of the buildings of a company, supervisors' salaries, leasing charges and insurance premiums.

Variable costs change in total in proprotion to changes in the related level of output so that the variable cost per unit remains the same if variable costs are represented by a straight line. Examples of short-term variable costs include piecework labo(u)r, direct materials and energy costs for the machines. Over a sufficiently long period of time virtually all costs of a company are variable.

Furthermore one must differentiate between direct costs and indirect costs, also called overheads. Direct costs are related to a specific cost object and are recorded by using vouchers. Examples of direct costs include tires and steering wheels for the production of cars. Special direct costs of sales and production can be assigned to a manufacturing or customer order but not to a particular product. They are also part of the product costing scheme. Examples of special direct costs include special tools and equipment, produced for one order and special carriage and promotion costs for a specific order or customer.

Indirect costs are not related to a particular unit of cost and are assigned to different cost centers by using a cost distribution sheet, an important tool of cost center accounting. Examples of indirect costs include insurance premiums and supervisors´ salaries, so these fixed costs are simultaneously indirect costs.

Questions and Tasks

1. List some costs which are simultaneously
   a. direct and variable
   b. indirect and variable
   c. indirect and fixed

2.2 Cost Element Accounting

Cost element accounting, also called cost type accounting, registers all the different cost elements within a period recorded by vouchers. There are several cost types which can arise in a cost center or in a cost object:

a. Personnel costs (e. g. wages, salaries, overtime payments, social security contributions, voluntary employee benefit expenses and severance payments).
   There are different kind of wages:
   - the time-rate wage, which is independent of the number of units produced and
   - the incentive wage, which is paid for piecework.

   The imputed entrepreneurial salary is important only for partnerships, i. e. private companies like sole proprietorships, general partnerships and limited partnerships. In these private companies, the general managers or the managing partners do not have a fixed salary as with corporations, i. e. limited (liability) companies, also called private limited companies, and public stock corporations, also called public (limited) companies.

b. Material costs (e. g. raw materials, operating supplies and manufacturing supplies). There are different inventory methods, e. g. the First-In First-Out (FIFO) method, the Last-In First-Out (LIFO) method and the average-cost method, in order to find the material costs.

c. Imputed depreciation: This refers to costs incurred in the wear and tear of fixed assets in consideration of their residual values. There are different depreciation methods, e. g. unit-of-production depreciation, straight-line depreciation, the declining-balance method of depreciation and the sum-of-the-years-digits method of depreciation. In cost accounting, manufacturing assets have to be written off against current replacement cost or current market value instead of acquisition cost or cost of goods manufactured, so that at the end of their service life, also called useful life, considering inflation, an equivalent asset with the same performance capability can be purchased in order to replace them.

Thus in cost accounting, often a higher degree of depreciation is needed than that permitted by the tax authorities. Therefore, in accounting, one must differentiate between depreciation for tax purposes and imputed depreciation for cost purposes. In Germany, only the latter is important in cost accounting, but in the US-GAAP regulations, only the balance sheet depreciation figures are taken into account in the cost of sales accounting method.

d. Imputed interest: These are imputed costs such as imputed depreciation and are also opportunity costs. Due to these costs, the company missed the opportunity to earn additional interest or income.

e. Imputed risk costs: These can arise from risks of storage, production, transportation etc., and can be deducted from the premiums of the insurance companies.

f. Outside services: These arise from services such as utilities, transportation, rent, lease, consulting etc.

Further important groups of cost elements are: repair costs, expenses for travel, hospitality, postage and telephone etc.

Questions and Tasks

1. What is the difference between
    a. raw materials
    b. operating supplies and
    c. manufacturing supplies?
    d. Give some examples of each of the materials above.

2. What is the difference between
    a. the FIFO method
    b. the LIFO method and
    c. the average cost method?

3. What is the difference between
    a. imputed depreciation and
    b. depreciation for tax purposes?

4. List some examples of
   a. social security contributions
   b. voluntary employee benefit expenses

5. Give some reasons for depreciation of goods.

2.3 Cost Center Accounting

2.3.1 What is Cost Center Accounting?

Cost center accounting gives information about each cost center's efficiency. It serves both as the cost center's planning and controlling tool and as a basis for the allocation rates for product costing. It shows where, i. e. in which cost center, costs have occured or may be expected. Moreover, cost center accounting is used to distribute indirect cost according to the casual relationship among the cost centers.

A cost center is the place where costs occur and is designated according to different criterions, such as:
   a. each cost center is an autonomous center of responsibility,
   b. each cost center's service must be clearly measured in activity units,
   c. all the vouchers of different costs can be easily associated with the casual cost centers.

There are manufacturing cost centers and cost centers for the issue of material, for the raw material warehouse, the distribution, the administration and eventually for research and development (R & D).

A cost distribution sheet is used in order to distribute only overhead expenses, the direct costs are not taken into account. Each line of this schedule contains one of the different cost elements, the cost centers are listed in the columns. Furthermore, a cost distribution sheet is used for the internal cost allocation, also called intracompany services charging. There are different methods to find the internal transfer prices.

2.3.2 Cost Allocation Methods

The emphasis of the following cost allocation methods is primarily on the allocation of indirect costs to divisions, plants, departments or contracts and secondarily to products and customers. Every contract with U.S. government agencies must comply with cost accounting standards issued by the Cost Accounting Standards Board, available from their website www.fedmarket.com.

Using the single-rate cost-allocation method in order to allocate costs from one department to another, there is no distinction between costs in terms of cost behaviour, such as fixed costs and variable costs, whereas the dual-rate cost-allocation method classifies costs into two subcost pools, a variable-cost subpool and a fixed-cost subpool.

Furthermore, a distinction must be made between operating departments, also called production departments in manufacturing companies, which add value to a product or service, and support departments, also called service departments, which provide services to operating departments and other support departments. Special cost-allocation problems result from support departments having provided reciprocal support to each other as well as support to operating departments.

Example:

	Support Departments		Operating Departments		Total
	A	B	C	D	
Overhead costs before inter-departmental cost allocation	$ 1 200 000	$ 232 000	$ 800 000	$ 400 000	$ 2 632 000
Support work by department A					
Labor-hours	250	550	1 200	2 000	4 000
Percentage	6.25 %	13.75 %	30 %	50 %	100 %
Support work by department B					
Labor-hours	40	10	400	50	500
Percentage	8 %	2 %	80 %	10 %	100 %
Units produced			2 000	5 000	

Now three different cost allocation methods will be examined in order to allocate the indirect costs of each support department using the single-rate method:

2.3.2.1 Direct Allocation Method

The direct allocation method, also called direct method, allocates the indirect costs of each support department directly to the operating departments, excluding its own use and the services provided to other support departments. Internal services between operating departments are also excluded.

	Support Departments		Operating Departments		Total
	A	B	C	D	
Overhead costs before inter-departmental cost allocation	$ 1 200 000	$ 232 000	$ 800 000	$ 400 000	$ 2 632 000
Allocation of department A	- $ 1 200 000	-	$ 450 000	$ 750 000	
Allocation of department B	-	- $ 232 000	$ 206 222	$ 25 778	
Total overhead of operating departments			$ 1 456 222	$ 1 175 778	$ 2 632 000
Overhead per unit produced			$ 728.11	$ 235.16	

The internal transfer price of one labor-hour of department A is calculated by dividing its overheads costs before any interdepartment cost allocations ($ 1 200 000) by the labor-hours worked in the operating departments (1 200 hours + 2 000 hours = 3 200 hours), i. e. $ 1 200 000 : 3 200 hours = $ 375 per hour. Both the amount of 250 hours of own use of department A and the amount of 550 hours of support time provided by department A to department B are excluded, because they are both support departments.

The internal transfer price of one labor-hour of department B is $ 232 000 : 450 hours = $ 515.56 per hour.

The overhead per unit produced is calculated as follows:
$ 1 456 222 : 2 000 units = $ 728.11 per unit produced in operating department C and
$ 1 175 778 : 5 000 units = $ 235.16 per unit produced in operating department D.

The direct allocation method is a simple way of allocating the indirect costs of support departments to the operating departments, but its results are not correct if there are any internal services between support departments, because these services are excluded.

2.3.2.2 Step-Down Allocation Method
(also called Sequential Allocation Method)

This method allows for partial recognition of the services rendered by support departments to other support departments. The support departments are ranked in the order that the step-down allocation is to proceed. Different sequences will result in different allocations of the costs of the ranked support departments
a. to support departments that render fewer services and
b. to operating departments.

The own use of each department is always excluded, internal services between operating departments can be excluded.

The step-down sequence begins with the support department that renders
a. the highest percentage of its total services or
b. the highest dollar amount of services
to other support departments.

The step-down sequence continues with the support department that renders
a. the next-highest percentage of its total services or
b. the next-highest dollar amount of services
to other support departments, and so on.

The sequence ends with the support department that renders
a. the lowest percentage of its total services or
b. the lowest dollar amount of services
to other support departments.

When the indirect costs of a support department have been allocated, no subsequent, lower ranked support department costs are allocated back to it, so that the total services that support departments provide to each other are not recognized.

	Support Departments		Operating Departments		Total
	A	B	C	D	
Overhead costs before interdepartmental cost allocation	$ 1 200 000	$ 232 000	$ 800 000	$ 400 000	$ 2 632 000
Allocation of department A	- $ 1 200 000	$ 176 000 $ 408 000	$ 384 000	$ 640 000	
Allocation of department B	-	- $ 408 000	$ 362 667	$ 45 333	
Total overhead of operating departments			$ 1 546 667	$ 1 085 333	$ 2 632 000
Overhead per unit produced			$ 773.33	$ 217.07	

The internal transfer price of one labor-hour of department A is calculated by dividing its overhead costs before any interdepartment cost allocations ($ 1 200 000) by the hours worked in support department B and in the operating departments C and D (550 hours + 1 200 hours + 2 000 hours = 3 750 hours), i. e. $ 1 200 000 : 3 750 hours = $ 320 per hour. The own use of 250 hours of department A is excluded.

The internal transfer price of one working hour of department B is $ 408 000 : 450 hours = $ 906.67 per hour. Both the amount of 10 hours own use of department B and the amount of 40 hours of support time provided by the lower ranked department B to department A are excluded.

The overhead per unit produced is calculated as follows:
$ 1 546 667 : 2 000 units = $ 773.33 per unit produced in operating department C and
$ 1 085 333 : 5 000 units = $ 217.07 per unit produced in operating department D.

2.3.2.3 Reciprocal Allocation Method

This method allocates indirect costs by explicitly including the mutual services provided among all support departments of a company and is therefore more accurate than the direct method and the step-down method.

Expressing the indirect costs and the reciprocal relationships of n support departments and operating departments will result in n linear equations:

I.	$ 1 200 000 +	250 A +	40 B	=	4 000 A
II.	$ 232 000 +	550 A +	10 B	=	500 B
III.	$ 800 000 +	1 200 A +	400 B	=	2 000 C
IV.	$ 400 000 +	2 000 A +	50 B	=	5 000 D

The 250 A term in equation I is the own use of 250 working hours of support department A, the 40 B term is the 40 working hours provided from support department B to support department A.

Solving the set of n linear equations by substituting an equation with another equation we obtain the complete reciprocated costs of each support department, which we allocate both to all other support departments and operating departments. If there are several support departments with reciprocal relationships, the calculation of the internal transfer prices and the overhead per unit produced can be made by using computer programs.

Substituting equation I with equation II we get:
II. $ 232 000 + 550 * (\$ 320 + \frac{4}{375} B) + 10 B = 500 B$
      $B = \$ 842.74$

Substituting with equation I we get:
I. $ \$ 1 200 000 + 250 A + 40 * \$ 842.74 = 4 000 A$
      $A = \$ 328.99$

The internal transfer price of one working hour of support departments A and B is A = $ 328.99 and B = $ 842.74.

The overhead per unit produced is $ 765.94 in operating department C and $ 220.02 in operating department D.

The reciprocal allocation method is not widely used because it is very complex.

The allocation of the support department costs according to the reciprocal method is as follows:

	Support Departments		Operating Departments		Total
	A	B	C	D	
Overhead costs before inter-departmental cost allocation	$ 1 200 000	$ 232 000	$ 800 000	$ 400 000	$ 2 632 000
Allocation of department A	$ 82 247.50	$ 108 944.50	$ 394 787	$ 657 980	
Allocation of Department B	$ 33 709.60	$ 8 427.40	$ 337 096	$ 42137	
Total overhead of operating Departments			$ 1 531 883	$ 1 100 117	$ 2 632 000
Overhead per unit produced			$ 765.94	$ 220.02	

Comparison of Cost Allocation Methods

The allocation of the two support departments' indirect costs using different cost allocation methods leads to the following results:

Cost Allocation Method	Internal transfer price of one labor-hour of support departments		Overhead per unit produced by operating departments	
	A	B	C	D
Direct method	$ 375	$ 515.56	$ 728.11	$ 235.16
Step-down method	$ 320	$ 906.67	$ 773.33	$ 217.07
Reciprocal method	$ 328.99	$ 842.74	$ 765.94	$ 220.02

Questions and Tasks

1. Cost Allocation

   The Miller Company has four departments. The two support departments are called A and B, the two operating departments are called C and D. Indirect costs incurred in the four departments for the first quarter of 2001 are as follows:

Department	Indirect Costs
A	$ 180 000
B	$ 682 500
C	$ 2 178 500
D	$ 2 929 000
Total	$ 5 970 000

   The mutual relationships among the four departments for the first quarter of 2001 are:

Labor-hours supplied by	Labor-hours used by				Total
	A	B	C	D	
A	100	150	350	400	1 000
B	200	50	250	500	1 000
Units produced			1 000	2 000	

   Allocate the two support department indirect costs to the two operating departments using
   a. the direct method,
   b. the step-down method,
   c. the reciprocal method.
   d. What ranking might be used to allocate support department costs when using the step-down method?
   e. Compare and explain differences in the allocation of the support department costs to the operating departments.
   f. Which cost allocation method might the Miller Company prefer? Why?

2.4 Product Cost Accounting

2.4.1 Product Costing Scheme

There are different types of cost objects, e. g. a single item, an order, a product, a service, a project etc. The idea of product costing is to find the cost of production per unit, the costs or the cost price per unit, the unit price and the profit per unit.

In order to find the costs of a product or service, a product costing scheme is often used which is based on the method of product costing with activity units and allocation rates, i. e. burden rates.

A distinction must be made between the process cost system and the overhead percentage cost calculation with its different allocation rates, e. g. material cost overhead rate, also called material handling charge and manufacturing overhead rate for an apportionment of indirect cost.

Product costing scheme:
    Direct material costs
+ Material overheads
+ Proportional manufacturing costs
+ Manufacturing overhead expenses
+ Special direct manufacturing costs
= Cost of production or manufacturing cost
+ Administrative costs
+ Sales and distribution costs
+ Special direct sales costs
= Cost price

2.4.2 Products of a Joint Production Process

Joint costs are the costs of a single production process that yields several products simultaneously. The distillation of coal, e. g., yields coke, natural gas and other products and the butchering of turkeys on a poultry farm yields breasts, thighs, drumsticks etc.

When a group of individual products is simultaneously produced, and each product has a relatively high sales value, the outputs are called joint products. When a joint production process yields only one product with a relatively high sales value, that product is called a main product. But those that have only a minor sales value when compared with the joint products are called by-products.

The split-off point is the specific point in a joint production process where one or more products become identifiable as different individual products.

The allocation of joint costs to individual products or services is sometimes required for inventory costing and cost-of-goods-sold computations, both for internal reporting purposes and reports for income tax authorities and for insurance settlement computations when damage claims are made.

The joint production costs before the split-off point cannot be distinctly identified with or traced to particular products, because the products themselves have not evolved before this point. The following joint-cost-allocation methods can be used both for costing the inventories and for determining cost of goods sold and can be divided into two categories:

1. methods for apportioning joint costs using physical-measure-based data such as weight or volume,
2. methods for apportioning joint costs using market-based data such as revenues:
   a. the sales value at split-off method,
   b. the net realizable value (NRV) method and
   c. the constant gross profit percentage method.

Using physical measure methods, the joint costs of the total production before the split-off point are allocated in proportion to volume, weight etc., so that each product is charged with its proportionate share of the joint costs.

Example:
Joint costs before the split-off point: $ 120 000.00
Further processing costs after the split-off point: $ 0.00

Product	Units produced	Joint costs allocated in proportion to units produced ($)	Sales value per unit ($)	Sales revenue ($)	Total cost ($)	Profit (loss) ($)
A	4 000	40 000	15.00	60 000	40 000	20 000
B	2 000	20 000	50.00	100 000	20 000	80 000
C	6 000	60 000	6.66	40 000	60 000	(20 000)
Total	12 000	120 000		200 000	120 000	80 000

Problems:
- In this example, the cost per unit, $ 120 000.00 : 12 000 = $ 10.00, is the same for each of the products, so that the stock valuations cost per unit of product C, $ 10.00, are higher than its market value per unit, $ 6.66.
- Furthermore, the stock valuations cost per unit are the same for each unit of the products A, B, and C, although they have different sales values per unit.

- Difficult measurement problems using this simple method arise if the different products consist of solids, liquids and gases and a common base must be found.

Using the sales value at split-off method, joint costs are allocated to joint products in proportion to the sales value for each of the products, so that a higher selling price indicates higher costs. In this method the sales value of the entire production of an accounting period is used, so that the joint costs are apportioned to all units produced, not just those sold in the current period.

Using the sales value at split-off method, joint costs are allocated as follows:

Product	Units produced	Sales value per unit ($)	Sales value ($)	Joint costs allocated in proportion to sales value ($)	Total cost ($)	Profit (loss) ($)
A	4 000	15.00	60 000	36 000	36 000	24 000
B	2 000	50.00	100 000	60 000	60 000	40 000
C	6 000	6.66	40 000	24 000	24 000	16 000
Total	12 000		200 000	120 000	120 000	80 000

Problems:
- The sales value at split-off method is based on the assumption that sales revenue determines prior costs, so that an unprofitable product with low sales revenue is allocated only a small share of joint costs, thus giving the impression that it is generating profits.
- Costs of an individual product caused by the production process beyond the split-off point are not taken into account.

Using the net realizable value method, all the further processing costs after the split-off point for each individual product are deducted from the respective sales value. The joint costs are allocated to joint products in proportion to the estimated net realizable value at the split-off point for each of the products produced during the respective period.

Product	Units produced	Sales value per unit ($)	Sales value ($)	Costs beyond split-off point ($)
A	4 000	15.00	60 000	16 000
B	2 000	50.00	100 000	20 000
C	6 000	6.66	40 000	4 000
Total	12 000		200 000	40 000

Product	Estimated net realizable value at split-off point ($)	Joint costs allocated in proportion to net realizable value at split-off point ($)	Profit (loss) ($)
A	44 000	33 000	11 000
B	80 000	60 000	20 000
C	36 000	27 000	9 000
Total	160 000	120 000	40 000

Using the constant gross profit percentage method, the joint costs of the total production are allocated to the joint products, so that the overall gross profit percentage is identical for every product, although such an assumption is questionable.

Product	Units produced	Sales value per unit ($)	Sales value ($)	Gross profit percentage; 40 000 (total profit) of 200 000 (total sales)
A	4 000	15.00	60 000	20 %
B	2 000	50.00	100 000	20 %
C	6 000	6.66	40 000	20 %
Total	12 000		200 000	20 %

Product	Gross profit (= total sales - total costs) ($)	Costs beyond split-off point ($)	Allocated joint costs ($)
A	12 000	16 000	32 000
B	20 000	20 000	60 000
C	8 000	4 000	28 000
Total	40 000	40 000	120 000

The joint costs allocated to each product need not always be positive using the constant gross profit percentage method, so that some products may receive negative allocations of joint costs just to bring their gross profit percentage up to the overall average of the products of the company.

Each company has its own predominant joint cost allocation method for stock valuation and profit measurement since each one has advantages. The advantages of the sales value at split-off method are the availability of a meaningful common denominator, the revenues, to compute the weighting factors and the simplicity of this method, especially in operations with multiple products and multiple split-off points.

2.4.3 Accounting for By-products

The joint costs should be charged to the joint and main products only, whereas the by-products should not be charged with any portion of the joint costs that are incurred before the split-off point. On the other hand, it is justifiable that only costs that are incurred in producing by-products after the split-off point can be charged to the by-product.

By-product revenues or by-product net revenues (i. e. the sales value of the respective by-product reduced by its further processing costs after the split-off point) should be deducted from the cost of the joint or main products of the production process. There are two different by-product accounting methods:

a. the production method recognizes by-products when they are produced and records by-product stocks at net realizable value plus separable manufacturing costs incurred,

b. the sale method recognizes by-products at the time of sale and records by-product stocks at their costs after the split-off point.

The production method leads to a premature recognition of profit, but because by-products are of a relatively minor sales value, their effects on the profits of the company are unimportant. Therefore, this method should be used if future sales are certain and the market price is stable, otherwise the sale method should be applied.

Example:

Product	Production for the period (units)	Sales for the period (units)	Opening stock (units)	Closing stock (units)	Price per unit ($)
Main product A	4 000	3 000	0	1 000	10.00
By-product B	800	400	0	400	2.00

Production costs before split-off point: $ 24 000.00
Production costs of by-product B beyond split-off point: $ 160
(= 800 units * $ 0.20 per unit)

Using the sale method, both the by-product closing stock of 400 units at $ 0.20 per unit and their production costs after the split-off point of $ 80.00 have been excluded, since their net effect is zero.

	Production method ($)	Sale method ($)
Sales revenue from main produt A (3 000 * $ 10.00)	30 000	30 000
Production costs of main product A	24 000	24 000
- Net realizable value from production of by-product B (800 * $ 1.80)	- 1 440	.
= Net production cost	22 560	24 000
- Closing stock of main product A (1/4) -	5 640	- 6 000
	16 920	18 000
- Net revenue from sale of by-product B (400 * $ 1.80)		- 720
= Cost of main product A sold	16920	17 280
Sales revenue from main product A	30 000	30 000
- Cost of main product A sold	- 16 920	- 17 280
= Gross profit	13 080	12 720

Further types of output which can result from a production process are:
- scrap, which is the leftover part of raw materials and can be sold or re-processed,
- waste, which is unsaleable and has no value or even negative value if it has to be disposed at some cost,
- defective units that do not meet common quality standards but can be rectified. Rectification should only be done if additional revenue will exceed additional costs.

2.4.4 Product Costing per Period

Product costing per period, also called period costing, is used in order to calculate the operating result of a company within a given period. Using the period accounting method all costs of a period must be subtracted from the revenue of this period in order to find the operating result. Using the cost of sales method all costs resulting from the units sold within a given period must be subtracted from their revenue in order to calculate the operating result. The cost of sales method requires cost element accounting, cost center accounting and product costing, because the results are shown according to products.

Questions and Tasks

1. Joint Products: Comparison of alternative Joint-Cost-Allocation Methods

   The Praefcke Company manufactures and distributes different chocolate products. There were no beginning inventories on October 1, 2003, and the entire output was sold to wholesalers. Production and sales data for October 2003 are:

Joint Products	Production (pounds)	Selling Price per Pound	Costs beyond Split-off Point
Happy Time	2 000	$ 3	$ 1 000
Sunshine	3 000	$ 8	$ 4 000
Super Power	5 000	$ 4	$ 5 000
Total	10 000		$ 10 000

   Calculate how the joint costs of $ 30 000 would be allocated to the three chocolate products using the following methods:
   a. Physical measure (pounds),
   b. Estimated net realizable value (NRV),
   c. Constant gross profit percentage.

2. Accounting for By-products

   The Farmer Company produces main product A and by-product B, which are fully processed at the split-off point, and there are no separable costs.

There were no opening stocks on November 1, 2003. Production and sales data for November 2003 are:

Production costs: $ 150 000

Product	Production (Units)	Sales (Units)	Selling Price per Unit
Main product A	20 000	18 000	$ 10
By-product B	4 000	3 000	$ 1

What is the gross profit under both methods of by-product accounting?

2.5 Cost-Volume-Profit (CVP) Analysis

2.5.1 Essentials of CVP Analysis

The CVP analysis is a systematic method of examining the behaviour of total revenues, total costs and operating income when changes occur in volume (i. e. the output level), selling price, variable costs per unit or fixed costs.

Total revenues can also be influenced by additional multiple revenue drivers (such as number of sales visits made to customers or number of advertisements placed), total costs can also be influenced by additional multiple cost drivers (such as number of batches in which units are produced), which are all not taken into account.

With every monopoly the total revenue line is curvilinear, because the company can only sell increasing quantities of output by reducing the selling price per unit, so that the total revenue line does not increase proportionately to the output. If the effect of price reductions outweighs the benefits of increased sales volume, the total revenue line begins to decline.

Total costs rise steeply as the company operates at the lower levels of output, at higher levels of output the total cost line rises less steeply. In the upper portion of the volume range the total cost line rises more and more steeply, because the machinery operates beyond the activity level for which it was designed and bottlenecks are thus caused.

If variable costs per unit are constant, the total cost function is linear. Step cost functions (i. e. step variable-cost functions and step fixed-cost functions) in which the cost remains the same over various levels of activity but the cost increases by discrete amounts as the level of activity changes from one range to the next, are not taken into account.

At the output level at which the difference between the total revenue and total cost lines is the greatest, the operating income of the company is at its maximum. At this point marginal revenue, which represents the increase in total revenue because of the sale of one additional unit, equals marginal costs, which represent the increase in total costs because of the production of one additional unit.

At output levels at which total costs are equal to total revenues, the operating income of the company is zero. These points are called break-even points.

At the output level at which total revenue reaches a maximum, marginal revenue is zero. The marginal cost curve reaches a minimum at the point of inflection of the total cost curve.

With every polypoly the selling price per unit is constant, so that the total revenue function is linear. If variable costs per unit are constant, too, and if variable costs per unit are lower than the selling price per unit, there is only one break-even point and the operating income widens as volume increases, so that the most profitable output is at maximum practical capacity.

The difference between total revenues and total variable costs of a company is its contribution margin. The contribution margin per unit is calculated as the difference between the selling price and the variable cost per unit.

Example:
Fixed costs: $ 1000.00
Selling price per unit: $ 15.00
Variable costs per unit: $ 10.00
Contribution margin per unit: $ 5.00

Units sold	0	100	200	300
Revenues ($)	0.00	1,500.00	3,000.00	4,500.00
- Variable costs ($)	0.00	1,000.00	2,000.00	3,000.00
= Contribution margin ($)	0.00	500.00	1,000.00	1,500.00
- Fixed costs ($)	1,000.00	1,000.00	1,000.00	1,000.00
= Operating income ($)	- 1,000.00	- 500.00	0.00 (= break-even point)	500.00

2.5.2 Mathematical Methods for Determining the Break-even Point

The break-even point tells managers what level of sales they have to generate to avoid a loss. The following abbreviations can be used to represent the various items in the subsequent equations:

OI = Operating income   x = Units sold
p = Unit selling price   a = Fixed costs
b = Unit variable costs   c = Unit contribution margin (= p - b)

2.5.2.1 Equation Method

Using this method the break-even point can be calculated by setting operating income in the following equation equal to zero:

Revenues - Fixed costs - Variable costs = Operating income
(p * x)   - a   - (b * x)   = OI

Using the information from the example above we obtain:

$ 15.00 * x - $ 1,000.00 - $ 10.00 * x = $ 0.00
                           $ 5.00 * x   = $ 1,000.00
                           x   = 200 units

If fewer than 200 units are sold, the managers will have a loss, if 200 units are sold, the operating income of the company is zero and if more than 200 units are sold, the managers will make a profit.

2.5.2.2 Contribution Margin Method

The contribution margin per unit is equal to the selling price per unit minus variable costs per unit. Using the information from the example above, the contribution margin per unit is $ 5.00, which is available to recover fixed costs and, after they are recovered, to increase operating income. The break-even point can be calculated by setting operating income in the following equation equal to zero:

Revenues - Fixed costs - Variable costs = Operating income
(p * x)   - a   - (b * x)   = OI
                          (p - b) * x   = OI + a
                          c * x   = OI + a
                          x   = $\frac{OI + a}{c}$

Setting OI = 0, we obtain x = (a : c).

Break-even point in units = (Fixed costs : Unit contribution margin).

In our example, fixed costs are $ 1,000.00 and the contribution margin per unit is $ 5.00, so that
break-even point in units = ($ 1,000.00 : $ 5.00 per unit) = 200 units.

2.5.2.3 Graph Methods

2.5.2.3.1 Cost-Volume-Profit Graph

The total costs line is the sum of the fixed costs and the variable costs. Fixed costs have always the same value at all output levels, measured on the y-axis. The fixed costs line is parallel to the x-axis. The total costs line intersects the fixed costs line at the point where the fixed costs line intersects the y-axis, because variable costs are $ 0.00 when 0 units are sold.

For the total revenues line one convenient starting point is $ 0.00 revenues when 0 units are sold.

The break-even point is the quantity of units sold at which total revenues equal total costs, so that the total revenues line and the total costs line intersect. At that point the operating income is zero. For quantities of sales less than the break-even point, total costs exceed total revenues, and the operating loss is indicated by the difference between the total costs line and the total revenues line. For quantities of sales greater than the break-even point, total revenues exceed total costs, and the operating income is indicated by the difference between the total revenues line and the total costs line.

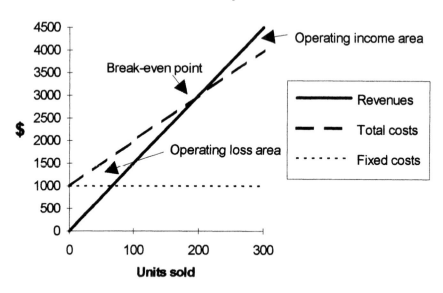

2.5.2.3.2 Profit-Volume Graph

This graph is helpful for answering the question of how many units a company has to sell to earn a given operating income, with a cost-volume-profit graph, on the other hand, it is not easy to determine the point at which the difference between the total revenues line and the total costs line is this specific value.

The profit-volume graph is a more convenient method of showing the impact of changes in the output level on operating income. The horizontal axis represents the various levels of sales volume, and the operating income is recorded on the vertical scale. The break-even point occurs at the point where the profit-volume line intersects the x-axis. At this point, the total contribution margin equals the total of the fixed costs. If sales are zero, the operating loss will be equal to the fixed costs.

To find the number of units a company has to sell to earn a certain operating income, draw a horizontal line corresponding to this specific value on the y-axis. At the point where this line intersects the profit-volume graph, a vertical line should be drawn to the x-axis. The vertical line intersects the x-axis at the number of units a company has to sell in order to generate this specific operating income.

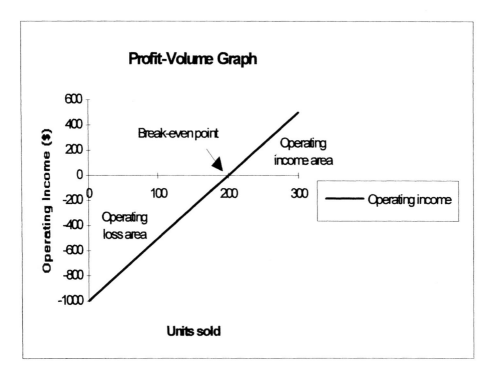

Questions and Tasks

Data of Blue Company for CVP Analysis
Fixed costs per annum: $ 100,000.00
Variable cost per unit: $ 40.00
Selling price per unit: $ 50.00
Existing sales: 15,000 units

1. What is the output level at which Blue Company generates an operating income of $ 0.00 (break-even point)?

2. How many units have to be sold to earn an operating income of $ 20,000.00?

3. What is the selling price which would have to be charged to earn an operating income of $ 125,000.00 on sales of 15,000 units?

4. What is the operating income that will result from a reduction of 10 % in variable costs and an increase of $ 30,000.00 in fixed costs?

2.6 What is the Difference between Variable Costing and Absorption Costing?

2.6.1 Introduction

Variable costing, also called direct costing or marginal costing, is a method of inventory costing which assigns only variable manufacturing costs to products. Consequently, only variable manufacturing costs are included as inventoriable costs, all fixed manufacturing costs are excluded and are treated as costs of the period in which they are incurred. Therefore this method should correctly be referred to as variable costing, because not all direct costs, e. g. direct labo(u)r, which can all be specifically identified with a product, may vary in the short term with changes in output.

Furthermore, the term marginal costing is also inappropriate, since marginal costs are the cost of producing one additional unit, so that fixed costs may being included, for instance due to the purchase of an additional machine.

Absorption costing, also called full costing, is a method of inventory costing in which both all variable manufacturing costs and all fixed manufacturing costs are allocated to products. Consequently, all variable manufacturing costs and all fixed manufacturing costs are included as inventoriable costs, since they are all regarded as product costs.

Both absorption costing and variable costing are similar with respect to all non-manufacturing costs, such as research and development and marketing, whether variable or fixed. They are considered as period costs. Thus, they are recorded as expenses when incurred and are therefore not inventoriable.

In the UK absorption costing is the required method of stock valuation for external reporting.

2.6.2 Calculating and Explaining Differences in Operating Income

To illustrate the difference between variable costing and absorption costing, let us have a look at the following illustration of both methods. The information is available for periods 1 - 6 for a company that manufactures and markets a single product:

	Periods					
	1	2	3	4	5	6
Opening stock (units)	0	0	20	0	0	70
Units produced	200	200	200	200	260	150
Units sold	200	180	220	200	190	200
Closing stock (units)	0	20	0	0	70	20

The following revenue and cost data which remain unchanged for periods 1 - 6:

Selling price $ 50.00   per unit sold
Variable manufacturing costs $ 10.00   per unit produced
Variable marketing costs (all indirect) $ 5.00   per unit sold
Fixed manufacturing costs (all indirect) $ 1,800.00   for each period
Fixed marketing costs (all indirect) $ 1,000.00   for each period

The normal activity for each period, which equals the budgeted denominator level of production, is 200 units.

The income statements for periods 1 - 6 using variable costing are as follows:

	Periods					
	1 ($)	2 ($)	3 ($)	4 ($)	5 ($)	6 ($)
Revenues	10,000	9,000	11,000	10,000	9,500	10,000
Variable costs						
Opening stock ($ 10 per unit)	0	0	200	0	0	700
+ Variable manufacturing costs ($ 10 per unit produced)	2,000	2,000	2,000	2,000	2,600	1,500
= Cost of goods available for sale	2,000	2,000	2,200	2,000	2,600	2,200
- Closing stock ($ 10 per unit)	0	200	0	0	700	200
= Variable cost of goods sold	2,000	1,800	2,200	2,000	1,900	2,000
+ Variable marketing costs ($ 5 per unit sold)	1,000	900	1,100	1,000	950	1,000
= Total variable costs	3,000	2,700	3,300	3,000	2,850	3,000
Contribution margin (= Revenues - Total variable costs)	7,000	6,300	7,700	7,000	6,650	7,000
Fixed costs						
Fixed manufacturing costs	1,800	1,800	1,800	1,800	1,800	1,800
+ Fixed marketing costs	1,000	1,000	1,000	1,000	1,000	1,000
= Total fixed costs	2,800	2,800	2,800	2,800	2,800	2,800
Operating income (= Contribution margin - Total fixed costs)	4,200	3,500	4,900	4,200	3,850	4,200

The income statements for periods 1 - 6 using absorption costing are as follows:

	Periods					
	1 ($)	2 ($)	3 ($)	4 ($)	5 ($)	6 ($)
Revenues	10,000	9,000	11,000	10,000	9,500	10,000
Cost of goods sold						
Opening stock ($ 19 per unit)	0	0	380	0	0	1330
+ Variable manufacturing costs ($ 10 per unit produced)	2,000	2,000	2,000	2,000	2,600	1,500
Fixed manufacturing costs ($ 9 per unit produced)	1,800	1,800	1,800	1,800	2,340	1,350
= Cost of goods available for sale	3,800	3,800	4,180	3,800	4,940	4,180
- Closing stock ($ 19 per unit)	0	380	0	0	1,330	380
+ Adjustments for under recovery of fixed overheads ($ 9 per unit)						450
- Adjustments for over recovery of fixed overheads ($ 9 per unit)					540	
= Cost of goods sold	3,800	3,420	4,180	3,800	3,070	4,250
Gross margin (= Revenues - Cost of goods sold)	6,200	5,580	6,820	6,200	6,430	5,750
Operating costs						
Variable marketing costs ($ 5 per unit sold)	1,000	900	1,100	1,000	950	1,000
+ Fixed marketing costs	1,000	1,000	1,000	1,000	1,000	1,000
= Total operating costs	2,000	1,900	2,100	2,000	1,950	2,000
Operating income (= Gross margin - Total operating costs)	4,200	3,680	4,720	4,200	4,480	3,750

In both systems (variable costing and absorption costing) all variable manufacturing costs are inventoriable costs. But under variable costing, fixed manufacturing costs are not inventoriable costs. Consequently, in this case they are treated as an expense of the period, whereas under absorption costing, fixed manufacturing costs are inventoriable costs. When using the absorption costing method, the fixed overheads are allocated to the units produced. In the example above, the fixed manufacturing overhead cost rate is $ 1,800 : 200 units = $ 9 per unit produced.

The total inventoriable costs per unit for periods 1 - 6 under the two methods are:

	Variable Costing	Absorption Costing
Variable manufacturing costs per unit	$ 10.00	$ 10.00
+ Fixed manufacturing costs per unit (all indirect)	-	$ 9.00
= Total inventoriable costs per unit	$ 10.00	$ 19.00

According to the table above, the closing stock is valued at $ 19 per unit ($ 10 variable manufacturing costs per unit + $ 9 fixed manufacturing costs per unit) in the absorption costing income statement, whereas the closing stock is valued at only $ 10 (variable manufacturing costs per unit) in the variable costing income statement. The units of closing stock become the opening stock for the respective following period and therefore an expense for this period.

The variable costing income statement uses the contribution margin; the fixed cost is charged separately. The absorption costing income statement uses the gross margin. Moreover, the distinction between manufacturing and nonmanufacturing costs is highlighted because the latter are charged separately. In the income statement under variable costing, the fixed manufacturing costs, a lump sum of $ 1,800 per period, are deducted as an expense for each of the periods 1 - 6.

Under absorption costing for the periods 1 - 4, the lump sum of $1,800 is treated as an inventoriable cost, possibly becoming a part of ending finished goods inventory. The $ 9 fixed manufacturing overhead cost rate per unit produced ($ 1,800 : 200 units) is based on a budgeted denominator level of 200 units produced per period, but in periods 5 and 6 the production deviates from the budgeted denominator level. The amount of fixed overheads, which has been charged too much or too little, is $ 9 multiplied by the difference between the actual level of production and the budgeted denominator level.

In period 5, fixed overheads of $ 540 too much has been charged ($ 2,330 instead of $ 1,800) due to the production of 260 units exceeding the budgeted denominator level of 200 units produced per period. This over recovery of fixed overheads is subtracted from the cost of goods available for sale (- adjustments for over recovery of fixed overheads, $ 540).

In period 6, fixed overheads of $ 450 too little has been charged ($ 1,350 instead of $ 1,800) due to the production of 150 units instead of 200 units produced per period. This under recovery of fixed overheads is added to the cost of goods available for sale (+ adjustments for under recovery of fixed overheads, $ 450).

If production is equal to sales in a period (here in periods 1 and 4) the operating income will be the same for both the absorption and the variable costing system. But if production is in excess of sales in a period (here in periods 2 and 5), the absorption costing system will show a higher operating income than the variable costing system. Therefore if stocks are increasing, under absorption costing an additional amount of fixed overheads (here $ 9 per unit) is deducted from the expenses of the respective period due to additional units in ending inventory.

If sales exceed production in a period (here in periods 3 and 6), the variable costing system will show a higher operating income than the absorption costing system. Therefore if stocks are declining, under absorption costing an additional amount of fixed overheads (here $ 9 per unit) is included as an expense and is charged for the respective period due to less units in ending inventory.

The difference between operating income under absorption costing and variable costing in a period can be calculated by the following two formulas:

1.
Absorption costing operating income
- Variable costing operating income

=

Fixed manufacturing costs in closing stock under absorption costing
- Fixed manufacturing costs in opening stock under absorption costing;

2.
Absorption costing operating income
- Variable costing operating income

=

Fixed manufacturing costs inventoried in units produced under absorption costing
- Fixed manufacturing costs of goods sold under absorption costing.

Because of increasing pressure on managers to reduce inventory levels in order to reduce storing charges, some companies have introduced just-in-time production. Consequently, these companies have less operating income differences between absorption costing and variable costing.

Under absorption costing, it can happen that the sales volume increases but operating income declines (see period 6), in spite of the fact that both the selling price and the cost structure have remained unchanged. This situation can arise if less is produced than budgeted, so that stocks decline strongly and a greater amount of fixed overheads is brought forward as an expense in the beginning inventory than it is being deducted in the ending inventory adjustment.

On the other hand, under absorption costing, it can happen that the sales volume declines but operating income increases (see period 5). This situation can arise due to more production than budgeted, so that stocks increase strongly and a smaller amount of fixed overheads is brought forward as an expense in the beginning inventory than it is being deducted in the ending inventory adjustment.

In contrast, under variable costing, operating income increases when the sales volume increases and when the sales volume declines, operating income declines, as well, as long as both the selling price and the cost structure remain unchanged. The period-to-period change in operating income under variable costing is calculated by the following formula:

   Contribution margin per unit
* <u>Period-to-period change in unit level of sales</u>
= Period-to-period change in variable costing operating income.

Consequently, the period-to-period change in operating income under variable costing is driven solely by changes in the unit level of sales, so that operating income cannot be increased by producing for inventory. In contrast, absorption costing enables managers to increase operating income by producing for inventory, since each additional unit in ending inventory will increase operating income by the respective fixed manufacturing costs per unit (here $ 9).

2.6.3 Advantages and Disadvantages of Absorption Costing

There are only a few and even so partially incorrect arguments in support of absorption costing. The most important one is:

Under absorption costing, fixed manufacturing costs are recorded as an expense only in the period in which the goods are sold. Therefore, large losses, especially in a business such as fireworks manufacturers, in which production is built up outside the sales season so that stocks are deliberately being built up to meet seasonal demand, are unlikely to be reported under absorption costing in the periods when stocks increase.

Although absorption costing is the required inventory method for external reporting in most countries, there are several arguments in support of variable costing for internal reporting:

a. Under variable costing methods the separation of fixed and variable costs helps to decide whether a component shall be produced internally or purchased externally. It also helps to estimate production costs for different levels of activities and to make pricing decisions.

b. Under variable costing, significantly fluctuating stock levels will not distort operating income, since only under absorption costing the stock level changes will affect the amount of fixed overheads charged to an accounting period. Thus, under variable costing for internal reporting, the internal income statements may be used as an appropriate basis for measuring managerial performance, since only when an absorption costing system is used managers may deliberately continually increase their inventory levels in order to influence operating income.

c. Under absorption costing, managers who want to increase operating income of the current period by producing for inventory may switch production to products that absorb the highest amount of fixed manufacturing costs per unit, regardless of the customer demand. Furthermore, they may defer maintenance beyond the current period, so that operating income of accounting periods in the future will probably decrease due to increased repairs and less efficient equipment.

d. Using an absorption costing system, stocks will be overvalued, especially when surplus stocks can only be disposed of when the previous selling price is reduced.

Consequently, it would be better to use variable costing instead of absorption costing for internal reporting, especially when there is no seasonal demand for the products of the respective company. Since stocks are unlikely to fluctuate very much from one accounting year end to the next, absorption costing should be used for external reporting, so that the annual profits represented in external accounting information are calculated according to a set of consistent accounting principles.

Some critics argue that only variable direct material costs are inventoriable costs, all other costs are costs of the period in which they are incurred. Therefore, they propose throughput costing, also called supervariable costing, to be used for internal reporting, but this method has not achieved widespread use by companies.

Other critics propose current cost accounting instead of historical cost accounting, so that stocks are valued at net realizable value or replacement cost rather than original acquisition cost. In this case, the absorption versus variable costing debate is no longer relevant.

Surveys of company practice in many countries report that the majority of the respondents even use absorption costing for internal profit measurement.

2.6.4 Combination of Absorption Costing and Variable Costing with Actual, Normal and Standard Costing

Both absorption costing and variable costing and also throughput costing may be combined with actual, normal or standard costing.

Actual costs have really occurred over a period and are recorded on the basis of vouchers, whereas normal costing is a costing method that allocates indirect costs based on the budgeted indirect cost rates multiplied by the actual quantity of the cost-allocation bases.

Both actual costing and normal costing trace direct costs to a cost object by using the actual direct-cost rates multiplied by the actual quantity of the direct-cost inputs. Using standard costing, direct costs are traced to a cost object by multiplying standard prices with the standard inputs allowed for actual outputs produced, whereas indirect costs are allocated on the basis of the standard indirect rates multiplied by the standard inputs allowed for the actual outputs produced.

The flexible budget, which shows the planned costs for the actual output, is calculated as follows:

(Actual activity * Proportional planned cost rate)
+ Planned fixed cost
= Flexible budget.

A variance analysis or a comparison of the budget with actual figures is used to compare the flexible budget and actual costs within a cost center.

2.6.5 Different Denominator-Level Capacity Concepts for Absorption Costing

There are four different denominator-level capacity concepts to determine the respective normal activity for each period, in order to calculate the fixed manufacturing overhead rate, which allocates fixed manufacturing costs to products under absorption costing:

a Theoretical capacity is based on producing at full efficiency and at maximum speed 24 hours a day with no interruptions, for instance due to maintenance.

b. Practical capacity corresponds to theoretical capacity reduced by unavoidable operating interruptions.

c. Normal capacity utilization is based on the level of capacity utilization that satisfies average customer demand over a time period of two to three years, taking seasonal, cyclical and trend factors into account.

d. Master-budget capacity utilization is based on the expected level of capacity utilization for only the next budget period, in general one year.

By using either theoretical capacity or practical capacity, it is calculated what a plant can supply, whereas when using normal capacity utilization or master-budget capacity utilization, demand is estimated. In most cases, the budgeted demand is below the production capacity available.

Example:

Budgeted fixed manufacturing costs per annum: $ 480,000.00

Denominator-Level Capacity Concept	Units	Budgeted Fixed Manu-facturing Overhead Rate per Unit	Variable Manu-facturing Cost per Unit	Total Manu-facturing Cost per Unit
Theoretical capacity	1,000,000	$ 0.48	$ 3.00	$ 3.48
Practical capacity	800,000	$ 0.60	$ 3.00	$ 3.60
Normal capacity utilization	600,000	$ 0.80	$ 3.00	$ 3.80
Master-budget capacity utilization	480,000	$ 1.00	$ 3.00	$ 4.00

Using the master-budget capacity utilization, the highest amount of fixed manufacturing costs per unit is assigned to each unit. Consequently, under absorption costing, the operating income is highest using the master-budget capacity utilization concept if inventory levels increase, and using the theoretical capacity concept if inventory levels decrease.

When using normal capacity utilization or master-budget capacity utilization, there is the danger of setting high, uncompetitive selling prices due to higher total manufacturing cost per unit, which results in a downward demand spiral:

A continuing reduction in demand can occur if the prices of competitors are not met so that demand drops, resulting in higher costs per unit.

There is no requirement for managers to use the same denominator-level capacity concept for controlling, external reporting and income tax purposes. However, for the latter, in the United States, the IRS requires companies to use only the practical capacity concept.

2.6.6 Stepwise Contribution Accounting

The contribution margin is calculated by subtracting variable costs from sales. The contribution margin per unit is equal to the selling price per unit minus the variable cost per unit.

The contribution margin per activity unit, e. g. hours or pieces, of a cost center is the relevant ratio if the available capacity of the respective cost center is what is causing the bottleneck. In this case, it is worth producing the goods with the highest contribution margin per activity unit.

Linear programming may be used if there are several simultaneous bottlenecks and if relationships can be assumed to be linear, i. e. the contribution margin per unit for each product and the utilization of resources per unit are the same whatever quantity of output is produced or sold.

Stepwise contribution accounting, an improvement of the variable costing, has several contribution margin steps, arising when different blocks of structure costs, i. e. fixed costs, are deducted from the contribution margin: first, structure costs of the product are deducted from the contribution margin I. From this result structure costs of the product group are deducted. Then, sales structure costs and other budgeted structure costs, e. g. administration structure costs are, deducted.

		Total company	Product group A			Product group B		
			Total A	A1	A2	Total B	B1	B2
	Sales							
-	Variable costs							
=	Contribution margin I							
-	Structure costs of the product							
=	Product contribution							
-	Structure costs of the product group							
=	Product group contribution							
-	Sales structure costs							
=	Sales contribution							
-	Other budgeted structure costs, e. g. administration structure costs							
=	Liquidity-related contribution							

Questions and Tasks

1. White Ltd is a company which manufactures and sells a single product at a selling price of $100.00 per unit. Its normal production level is 1,000 units per annum. Data relating to 2001, 2002 and 2003 are shown in the following table:

	2001	2002	2003
Beginning inventory (units)	0	100	300
Units produced	1,000	1,200	800
Units sold	900	1,000	1,050

Cost data which remain unchanged are:
Variable manufacturing costs per unit produced $25.00
Variable operating costs (all indirect) per unit sold $10.00
Fixed manufacturing costs (all indirect) per annum $20,000.00
Fixed operating costs (all indirect) per annum $12,000.00.

a. Prepare income statements for White Ltd for 2001, 2002 and 2003 under
   - variable costing and
   - absorption costing.

b. Explain the difference in White Ltd's operating income for each of the three years under variable costing and absorption costing.

c. Explain why White Ltd's operating income for 2003 is less than for 2002 under absorption costing even though sales have increased in 2003.

d. Is variable costing or absorption costing more likely to lead to excessive inventory buildups? Why?

2. Green Company purchased a plant, having budgeted fixed manufacturing costs of $ 12 million in 2005. You are required to decide on the denominator-level concept to use in your absorption costing system for 2005:

Denominator-Level Capacity Concept	Units	Variable Manufacturing Cost per Unit
Theoretical capacity	4,000,000	$ 36.00
Practical capacity	3,000,000	$ 36.00
Normal capacity utilization	2,000,000	$ 36.00
Master-budget capacity utilization	1,500,000	$ 36.00

Beginning inventory: 500,000 units
Selling price: $ 45.00 per unit sold

a. Calculate the budgeted fixed manufacturing overhead rate per unit and the total manufacturing cost per unit using each of the four denominator-level capacity concepts under absorption costing.

b. Which denominator-level capacity concept should the manager prefer if he wants to maximize the operating income in 2005, neglecting fixed and variable marketing costs if

   b_1. actual production is 2,500,000 units and actual sales are 2,000,000 units in 2005,

   b_2. actual production is 2,000,000 units and actual sales are 2,500,000 units in 2005?

Chapter 3: Economics

3.1 Vocational School, Apprenticeship and Banking

Antje and Vera are two trainees. They started their apprenticeship in catering two months ago, so their probationary period will end next month. Up to that time they can be dismissed any time for no reason at all without notice since they don't have any protection against dismissal. At the same time they can also give notice during this period for no reason, too. The notice must be written, not oral. Today they will meet each other at the vocational school.

Antje: I've just come from the resident's registration office. I've been living with my boyfriend in a new flat since Monday. In the application form I had to fill in so many words and syllables. They asked me whether I was widowed or divorced, and they needed a specimen signature. Every month we have to pay 150.00 euros each for the flat. We have a joint account, so we are both account holders and have the authority to sign each. We pay the rent by standing order and have an overdraft facility of 3,000.00 euros but we don't want to overdraw our account.

Vera: I've bought a new car, a Lupo; however I would like to have bought a Porsche. Those are the best cars in the world. In a market survey they found out that these cars have an outstanding value for the money and less wear and tear so the depreciation is low. We bought the Lupo at a subsidiary of the pan-European company where my boyfriend is employed. This company is not subsidized by the German state.

Antje: Did you read the General Business Conditions and the small print in the sales contract?

Vera: Oh, yes. We couldn't pay cash, so we are paying in installments, including a handling charge of 60.00 euros.

Antje: O.K., payment on an open account thirty days after delivery is unusual if you buy a car. But I hope that you will never default because they don't accept deferred payment.

Vera: Oh, no! I don't want to pledge the car or pay a penalty fee or penalty interest.

Antje: Don't worry, first of all you get a reminder. Yesterday, I wanted to get a statement of my account out of the statement printer, but the magnetic strip of my Eurocheque card was defective, so I don't know my account balance. I hope I am not in the red, because I've made so many withdrawals. I don't want them to seize my car and auction it off.

Vera: I always have too little money in my purse and my account is always debited, as well.

Antje: The new notes from the European Central Bank (ECB) are especially tamper-proof and can not be easily forged, so I hope that the purchasing power of this new currency will be stable. I always have too few euros since I've been put into the first tax bracket and have to declare a high percentage of my income.

Vera: Of course the gross income is always much higher than the net income, and I wish I was taking the gross income home.

Antje: I know what you mean. Let's buy something to eat, I'm getting hungry.

Vera: Me too, by the way, don't forget to watch out for the expiry date, otherwise you can't claim compensation. We should buy some clothes, too, because the seasonal sales start today. After shopping I'll buy some shares of Infenion. I've seen the ads for the IPO.

Antje: What is an IPO?

Vera: IPO stands for initial public offering. That's when a new company is floated and its shares are launched onto the market. The company was floated on the stock market one week ago and the fluctuation of its shares is enormous.

Antje: Thanks, now I understand. There are so many companies in the Neuer Markt, like Edel Music which started life in 1986 as small mail order business. In the Neuer Markt so many share prices are fluctuating and the glut of information makes it hard to sift the wheat from the chaff. Is it free of charge to buy and sell shares?

Vera: No, but my boyfriend has placed a lot of new shares in his existing portfolio. If he can save a lot of money, he'd like to become self-employed and an entrepreneur. He always says he wants to raise the GDP (gross domestic product) and the GNP (gross national product). If the operating costs of his company are low, he can offer good prices and be more competitive. If he makes a lot of money, he will buy a big house because he likes investing in real estate.

Antje: I hope he'll grant me a discount and a better grace period if I make a sales contract with him. But does he have enough money at his disposal?

Vera: I don't think so, but I am not sure because I don't have any basic data about his company. I'm sure that he'll give his first customer's reference number to me. I think he will have no problems with his bank and with Standard & Poors, the credit reference agency.

Antje: How are these loans secured?

Vera: They often register land-charges against my property or ask for guarantees.

Antje: Will you be a guarantor for his credit, too?

Vera: No, he'll have to be careful about the credit and the repayment if he works on his own. I can only help him with the statutes of his company.

Antje: What is the interest rate right now?

Vera: At the moment the annual percentage rate (APR) is 5.25 % on loans of up to 10 years; 96 % of the loan amount will be paid out, so the true interest rate (true APR) is 6.18 %.

Antje: O.K. Now let's prepare for the next class-test on monetary and fiscal policy, tangible and intangible assets, economy of scale, free-market ideology, data privacy and money laundering so that we can get good marks on the tests and on our report cards.

Questions and Tasks

1. How much is the minimum and the maximum of the probationary period during an apprenticeship?
2. Someone started his traineeship on the 1st August 1995. His final test was on the 17th June 1998. When will his traineeship end?
3. Somebody wants to work in another company after his traineeship. Does he have to give notice after his final test?
4. What is the difference between a notice during and after the probationary period?
5. How many vocational schools are in your town?
6. What are the different types of personal status?
7. Discuss the pros and cons of a joint account.
8. What is the difference between payment by standing order and payment by direct debit?
9. To whom would you give a direct debit authorization?
10. Which different means of payment do you know?
11. Which different methods of payment do you know?
12. Does your company have any subsidiaries?
13. Which companies or lines of business are subsidized by the German government? Why are they subsidized?
14. Give some reasons for depreciation.
15. What do the General Business Conditions govern? Give examples.
16. Which products do you have to pay for
    - in advance
    - on open account
    - in cash
    - in installments?
17. Which goods can't be pledged?
18. Which features make the new notes tamper-proof and a forgery difficult?
19. How many tax brackets does the German tax system have? What are their differences?

20. Where are headquarters of the European Central Bank (ECB)? What is the name of its president?
21. List some countries and their currencies which have a low purchasing power. Why is their purchasing power low?
22. What kind of things belong to real estsate?
23. How has the Neuer Markt developed since its launch in 1997?
24. What sort of investors does the Neuer Markt attract?
25. List further indexes like the Nemax 50.
26. In what kind of businesses are the Neuer Markt companies specialized?
27. List some companies which offer their shares on the stock exchange. Why do they issue shares?
28. Where are stock exchanges in Germany located?
29. What is the difference between the GDP and the GNP?
30. What is the difference between the real and the nominal GDP and between the real and the nominal GNP?
31. What kind of features can influence the price range of a product?
32. How many figures does the customer's reference number of your company have?
33. What do the articles of association govern?
34. Why is the APR lower than the true APR?
35. What is the difference between monetarism and fiscalism?
36. List some intangible assets.
37. Which subjects are on your report card in your vocational school?
38. How can economies of scale be realized?
39. List some location factors.
40. When will the receivables expire under statute of limitations if you buy a car and don't pay the installments?
41. List some statutory limitation periods and give examples for statutes of limitation.

3.2 Quantitative Models for the Planning, Management and Control of Stocks

3.2.1 Introduction

A lot of companies produce a wide range of products requiring many components and parts. Therefore, the problems of planning, managing and controlling materials in these businesses, e. g. to determine optimum stock levels and economic order quantities, are very complex.

When determining optimum stock levels, production requirements and customer demand should always be met but excessive stocks have to be avoided because unnecessary money is tied in stocks and goods can be spoiled. Furthermore it should be taken into account that your company can cover an underestimated customer demand. If it is expected that future prices of input factors rise significantly, a company should consider increasing its stocks in the case that future cost savings due to currently lower purchase prices are higher than the increased costs due to holding additional stocks.

In addition one must determine both the stock level at which materials should be replenished, i. e. the re-order point, and the quantity to be ordered, i. e. the re-order quantity. Stock records of the quantity of material in stock are kept on a bin card or on a computer.

Bin Card								
Article no.:			Maximum:			Normal quantity to order:		
Article name:			Minimum:			Re-order level:		
Receipts			Issues			Balance		
Date	GRN no. *	Quantity	Date	Req. no.	Quantity	Quantity	Signature	Remarks

* GRN = goods received note

When items of materials have reached the re-order point, a purchase requisition, written on a purchase movements card, is sent to the purchasing department, so that the re-order quantity can be bought from the appropriate supplier. The information about the different suppliers of each individual item of materials are recorded on a purchase stock card.

After the goods are received, inspected and checked with the supplier's delivery note and a copy of the purchase order by the stores department, the accounts department will settle the invoice for the goods received. The information on quantity and value of each individual item of materials in store is recorded in a stores ledger account.

colspan="11"	**Stores ledger account**
Article no.:				Maximum:				Normal quantity to order:		
Article name:				Minimum:				Re-order level:		
	Receipts				Issues				Stock			
D.	GRN no.	Q.	U. p. ($)	A. ($)	D.	Req. no.	Q.	U. p. ($)	A. ($)	Q.	U. p. ($)	A. ($)	Sig.	Rem.

D. = date   Q. = quantity   U. p. = unit price
A. = amount   Sig. = signature   Rem. = remarks

3.2.2 Economic Order Quantity

In order to calculate the relevant costs when determining optimal stock levels, one must distinguish between holding costs and ordering costs.

Holding costs consist of the following items:
a. opportunity cost due to the investment in stocks,
b. incremental costs, e. g. insurance, warehouse, storage and material handling costs,
c. cost due to obsolescence and deterioration of stocks.

Ordering costs normally consist of the clerical costs of preparing purchase orders, sending them to the suppliers, receiving deliveries and settling invoices. If there are no quantity discounts, acquisition costs are not included in the quantitative models, because they remain unchanged, irrespective of the order size of total annual requirements.

If less units are ordered at one time, more orders are necessary in order to purchase the total annual requirements. This will result in an increase in the ordering costs, but on the other hand, lower average stocks must be maintained, which leads to a decrease in holding costs. The optimum order size, also called economic order quantity, is the order quantity that will result in the sum of the ordering and holding costs being minimized and can be determined by using
a. the tabulation method,
b. the graphical method or
c. the formula method,
which are now described:

Example:
Total annual demand (D):   3,600 units
Purchase price per unit: $ 100.00
Annual holding costs per unit (H): $ 20.00
Cost per purchase order (O): $ 10.00
Base stock (= safety stock) (B):   20 units

Assumptions:
- The holding costs per unit will always be constant.
- A constant amount of stock is used per day (no seasonal and cyclical factors).
- The size of the base stock is irrespective of the order quantity.

3.2.2.1 Tabulation Method

The annual relevant costs for different order quantities are listed in the following table. The number of purchase orders per year is calculated by dividing the total annual demand by the order quantity. The average stock in units is determined by the sum of one-half of the quantity ordered and the base stock in units. The annual holding cost is calculated by multiplying the average stock in units by the annual holding cost per unit.

Order quantity	Number of purchase orders per year	Annual ordering cost ($)	Average stock in units	Annual holding cost ($)	Total relevant cost ($)
20	180	1,800	30	600	2,400
40	90	900	40	800	1,700
60	60	600	50	1,000	1,600
80	45	450	60	1,200	1,650
100	36	360	70	1,400	1,760

The economic order quantity, at which the sum of annual ordering and holding costs is at a minimum, is 60 units.

3.2.2.2 Graphical Method

The x-axis represents the order quantities, the y-axis represents the annual costs. If the order quantity increases, the holding costs also increase, whereas the ordering costs decline. The economic order quantity is 60 units. At this point the total cost line is at a minimum.

If there is no base stock, the economic order quantity, where the total cost line is at a minimum, can be found at the point where the holding costs equal the ordering costs.

Determining the Economic Order Quantity

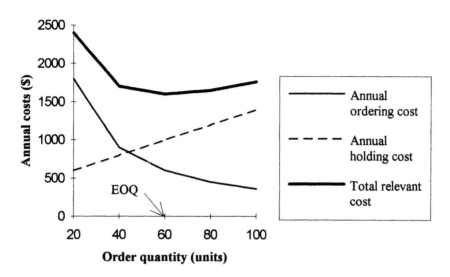

3.2.2.3 Formula Method

$$\text{Number of orders} = \frac{\text{total demand for period}}{\text{quantity ordered}} = \frac{D}{Q}$$

$$\text{Total ordering costs (TOC)} = \frac{\text{total demand for period} * \text{ordering costs per order}}{\text{quantity ordered}}$$

$$= \frac{D*O}{Q}$$

$$\text{Average stock for the period} = \frac{\text{quantity ordered}}{2} + \text{base stock } (B) = \frac{Q}{2} + B$$

Total holding costs per period (THC) = ((quantity ordered)/2 + base stock) * holding costs per unit per period (H)

$$= (Q/2 + B) * H$$

Total costs (TC) = total ordering costs (TOC) + total holding costs (THC)

$$= \frac{D*O}{Q} + \left(\frac{Q}{2} + B\right) * H$$

In order to find the economic order quantity Q, the minimum of the total cost function (TC) is determined by differentiating the above formula wih respect to Q and setting the first derivative equal to zero:

$$Q = \sqrt{\frac{2 * total \cdot demand \cdot for \cdot period * cost \cdot per \cdot order}{holding \cdot cost \cdot per \cdot unit}}$$

$$= \sqrt{\frac{2*D*O}{H}}$$

Applying this formula to the example above, the economic order quantity

$$Q = \sqrt{\frac{2*3{,}600*10}{20}} = 60 \text{ units.}$$

3.2.3 Economic Order Quantity with Respect to Quantity Discount

If companies are able to obtain quantity discounts for large purchase orders, the cost savings due to

a.) a saving in purchase price for the total demand of the period and
b.) a reduction in the total ordering costs due to fewer orders based on larger order quantities

must be balanced against the increased holding costs, when the economic order quantity is calculated.

Example:
Total annual demand (D):   3,600 units
Purchase price per unit: $ 100.00
Annual holding cost per unit (H): $ 20.00
Cost per purchase order (O): $ 10.00
Base stock (B):   0 units
Quantity discount: 2 % of the purchase price
Order quantity to obtain the discount (Q_D): 100 units

$$\text{Economic order quantity (Q)} = \sqrt{\frac{2*3{,}600*10}{20}} = 60 \text{ units}$$

Should the company order in batches of 100 units in order to obtain quantity discounts for larger order sizes?

If the company purchases in batches of 100 units instead of batches of 60 units, the cost savings are as follows:

a.) Savings in purchase price for the total annual demand:
= 3,600 * $ 100.00 * 2 % = $ 7,200.00

b.) Savings in ordering costs:
$$= \frac{D*O}{Q} - \frac{D*O}{Q_D}$$

$$= \frac{3{,}600 * \$10.00}{60} - \frac{3{,}600 * \$10.00}{100}$$

$$= \$600.00 - \$360.00 = \$240.00$$

Total cost savings = $ 7,200.00 + $ 240.00 = $ 7,440.00

The additional holding cost arising from higher stock levels when larger quantities are purchased is calculated as follows:

$$\frac{(Q_D - Q) * H}{2} = \frac{(100 - 60) * \$20.00}{2} = \$400.00$$

The company should adopt the quantity of 100 units, since the cost savings of $ 7,440.00 exceed the additional holding costs of $ 400.00. If, furthermore, larger discounts are available for larger order sizes, an additional, similar analysis should be applied for this order quantity.

3.2.4 Determining the Re-order Point and other Stock Figures

Re-order point: the point in time at which an order for materials, components etc. should be placed in order to obtain additional stocks.

Lead time: the time that elapses between placing an order and the delivery of the ordered goods.

Safety stock: Stock maintained in order to protect a company from condi-
(= base stock) tions of uncertainty, e. g. demand and lead time, and to avoid stockout costs, e. g. loss of contribution, stoppage in production, idle time.

Re-order point = safety stock + (lead time * daily usage)

Maximum stock: the largest quantity of goods which a company can store at one time.

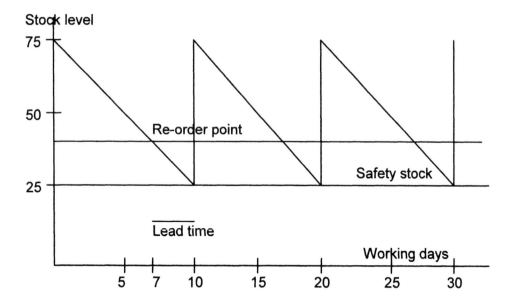

Example:
Safety stock: 25 units Working days per year: 200
Lead time: 3 days Purchase price per unit: $ 100.00
Daily usage: 5 units Annual holding cost per unit: $ 4.00
                                     Cost per purchase order: $ 5.00

Total annual demand = 5 units per day * 200 working days per year
                           = 1,000 units

Economic order quantity $= \sqrt{\dfrac{2*1,000*5}{4}} = 50$ units

Re-order point = 25 + (3 * 5) = 40

Average stock in units = (50 : 2) + 25 = 50

Turnover rate $= \dfrac{\text{Total annual demand}}{\text{Average stocks in units}} = \dfrac{1000}{50} = 20$

Average time of storage $= \dfrac{360 \text{ days}}{\text{Rate of turnover}} = \dfrac{360 \text{ days}}{20} = 18$ days

3.2.5 ABC Classification Method

In large companies with thousands of different items to be stored, it is essential that these materials are classified into categories of importance so that these companies can apply the most elaborate procedures of planning, managing and controlling stocks only to the most important items.

Managers have to estimate the quantity and the total purchase cost for each item of stock for the period based on the sales forecast for the products of the company. Then the items are grouped in decreasing order of annual purchase cost.

Between 5 and 15 % of the items in stock represent between 70 and 80 % of the total annual purchase cost. These items are categorized as A items, and the quantitative models for the control of stocks are applied to the A-category items so that the company maintains low safety stocks consistent with the avoidance of high stockout costs.

The next 10 or 20 % of items in stock are classified as B items, for which the quantitative methods for the control of stocks are not as sophisticated as for the A-category items. These items represent between 10 and 20 % of the total annual purchase cost.

The final 70 or 80 % of items in stock, representing only approximately 5 or 10 % of the total annual purchase cost, are categorized as C items. Larger order quantities, stocks and safety stocks are features of the C-category items, for which re-order points are determined only on a subjective basis in order to minimize the expense in controlling these items.

Example:

Item	Estimated usage per year (units)	Unit price ($)	Total annual purchase cost ($)	Rank balanced on total annual purchase cost
I	3,000	6.00	18,000.00	1
II	11,000	0.10	1,100.00	4
III	2,000	1.05	2,100.00	3
IV	20,000	0.04	800.00	5
V	4,000	0.75	3,000.00	2
Total	40,000		25,000.00	

Item based on rank	Estimated usage per year		Total annual purchase cost		Category based on ABC classification method
	units	%	$	%	
I	3,000	7.5	18,000.00	72.0	A
V	4,000	10.0	3,000.00	12.0	B
III	2,000	5.0	2,100.00	8.4	B
II	11,000	27.5	1,100.00	4.4	C
IV	20,000	50.0	800.00	3.2	C
Total	40,000	100,0	25,000.00	100.0	

Category based on ABC classification method	Estimated usage per year		Total annual purchase cost	
	units	%	$	%
A	3,000	7.5	18,000.00	72.0
B	6,000	15.0	5,100.00	20.4
C	31,000	77.5	1,900.00	7.6
Total	40,000	100.0	25,000.00	100.0

Category based on ABC classification method	Estimated usage per year (cumulative)		Total annual purchase cost (cumulative)	
	Units	%	$	%
A	3,000	7.5	18,000.00	72.0
B	9,000	22.5	23,100.00	92.4
C	40,000	100.0	25,000.00	100.0

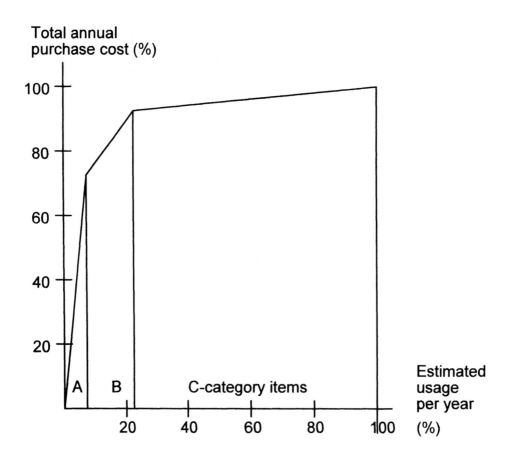

Questions and Tasks

1. Blue Company uses 9,000 units of material per year and the purchase price is $ 100 per unit. Costs per purchase order are $ 45, annual holding costs per unit are $ 9.

   Working days per year: 200   Base stock: 450 units
   Daily usage: 45 units   Lead time: 5 days

   a. Determine the economic order quantity using
      - the tabulation method,
      - the graphical method and
      - the formula method.

   b. The supplier offers a quantity discount of 10 % if Blue Company purchases in batches of 500 units. Should Blue Company order in batches of 500 units in order to obtain quantity discounts?

   c. Determine
      - the re-order point,
      - the average stock in units,
      - the rate of turnover and
      - the average time of storage.

2. Green Company has different items in stock:

Item	Estimated usage per year (units)	Unit price ($)
I	5,000	4.00
II	15,000	0.20
III	9,000	2.00
IV	18,000	0.50
V	3,000	50.00
Total	50,000	

   Determine the category of each item in stock using the ABC classification method.

3.3 Benchmarking

Benchmarking is an analysis and planning tool for comparing the products, services, activities and results of a company with the performance of the best of the competing enterprises in order to discover opportunities for rationalization or for improving quality and performance. Furthermore, comparisons with the best of other organizations having similar processes or with the best companies of other lines of business are made.

Important items in benchmark comparisons are unit cost, revenue, gross margin, labor cost, customer satisfaction etc., and the main task is to examine <u>why</u> the observed differences exist for all companies.

Questions and Tasks

1. List further items used in benchmark comparisons.
2. List some problems which can arise using benchmarks.

3.4 Office Equipment

Match these words with the definitions below:

A adhesive tape	J folder	S pointer
B calculator	K fountain pen	T punch
C carbon paper	L glue	U rubber (= eraser)
D cartridge	M guillotine	V ruler
E date stamp	N ink-pad	W staple
F drawing pin	O (pair of) compasses	X stapler
G envelope	P (pair of) scissors	Y transparency
H file	Q paper clip	Z typewriter
I filing cabinet	R pencil sharpener	

1   holder, box etc. for storing several sheets of paper
2   place to store files
3   elastic material for correcting words or digits written by pencil
4   machine for calculating figures
5   object used for printing dates on the surface of letters, e. g. when they are received
6   instrument for cutting sheets of paper
7   device made of metal for tacking sheets of paper together and which can be removed easily
8   instrument for sharpening blunt pencils
9   instrument for cutting holes in sheets of paper so that they can be put in a holder
10 tool for drawing straight lines and measuring lengths
11 tool with two blades for cutting paper etc.
12 hand-operated instrument for tacking sheets of paper together
13 U-shaped object made of metal and filled in a stapler
14 object for ink used on rubber stamps
15 machine which was replaced by computers
16 transparent object on which one can write and sketch in order to present by using an overhead projector
17 sticky, thick liquid paste for sticking something onto a place where it should not easily be removed
18 device for sticking something onto a place so that it can be easily removed
19 tool for fixing notes written on a sheet of paper onto a notice-board
20 wrapper, made mostly of paper, for finished letters
21 V-shaped instrument made of metal for drawing circles of different sizes
22 paper, used between sheets of writing paper for making a duplicate
23 pen filled with ink-filled cartridges
24 holder for storing a few, loose sheets of paper
25 object filled with ink
26 stick used for emphasizing things on a chart while making presentations

3.5 Capital Investment Decisions

3.5.1 Discounted Cash Flow (DCF) Methods

Discounted cash flow methods focus on cash inflows and outflows rather than on operating income. They measure all expected future cash inflows and outflows of each project of a company as if they occurred at a single point in time, although a significant period of time elapses between the outlay, e. g. acquisition cost, and the recoupment of the investment.

The interest cost, which is an opportunity cost, resulting from the commitment of funds for a significant period of time and the discount rate, which is the minimum acceptable rate of return on an investment, need not be ignored in this analysis. Capital investment decisions are important for every company, because they tie a substantial proportion of the resources of the enterprise to actions that are likely to be irreversible.

For reasons of simplification, we will use the following assumptions:
a. all cash inflows and outflows of each project are known with certainty,
b. sufficient funds are available for the company to undertake all profitable investments,
c. taxes and inflation are ignored,
d. the cost of capital, e. g. the discount rate, is constant,
e. all capital projects have an equal risk and
f. all expected future cash inflows and outflows of each project will occur at the end of the year.

A company should invest in capital projects only if it yields a percentage return on investment, the marginal revenue, which exceeds the discount rate of the investment, the marginal cost of capital.

3.5.1.1 Net Present Value (NPV) Method

The net present value of an investment is the discounted present value of all expected future cash inflows less the discounted present value of the outflows of this project. Only projects with a positive net present value should be accepted, since the return from these investments exceeds the cost of capital. A zero NPV indicates that the company should be indifferent to whether the investment is accepted or the capital is invested elsewhere. Projects with a negative NPV should be rejected. If the risk of each investment is equal, the higher the respective NPV, the better the investment.

The NPV is calculated as follows:

$$NPV = \frac{FV_1}{(1+K)^1} + \frac{FV_2}{(1+K)^2} + \ldots + \frac{FV_n}{(1+K)^n} - I_0$$

FV_n = future value of an investment in n years
n = number of years
K = discount rate
I_0 = initial investment cost, e. g. acquisition cost, invested at the beginning of the project in year 0

Example:
Initial investment cost: $ 500 000
Useful life: 3 years
Discount rate: 10 %

Year	Annual cash inflow ($)
1	200 000
2	500 000
3	60 000

The NPV calculation of the investment is

$$NPV = \frac{\$200\,000}{(1.1)^1} + \frac{\$500\,000}{(1.1)^2} + \frac{\$60\,000}{(1.1)^3} - \$500\,000 = \$140\,120$$

Alternatively, each year's cash flow can be discounted separately using a published table of present value factors (see Appendix, Table 1). There the discount factors can be found by referring to each year of the cash inflows and the discount rate. Each year's cash flow should be multiplied by the appropriate discount factor in order to calculate the present value of the cash flows:

Year	Annual cash inflow ($)	Discount factor (discount rate = 10 %)	Present value ($)
1	200 000	0.909090	181 818
2	500 000	0.826446	413 223
3	60 000	0.751315	45 079

	640 120
- Initial investment cost ($)	500 000
= NPV ($)	140 120

The discount factor of the year n is calculated by the formula $1 : (1 + K)^n$. The project should be accepted, because its NPV is positive.

Only if the investment produces an annuity, i. e. when the annual cash flows are the same each year, the present value of the cash flows can be calculated by multiplying the annual cash inflow by the appropriate cumulative present value factors, which is the sum of each year's discount factors for the period of the project and which is also published in tables (see Appendix, Table 2).

Example:
Initial investment cost: $ 800 000
Useful life: 3 years
Discount rate: 10 %

Year	Annual cash inflow ($)
1	500 000
2	500 000
3	500 000

The NPV is calculated as follows:

Annual cash inflow * Discount factor = Present value
(n = 3 years, discount rate = 10 %)

$ 500 000   * 2.486852   = $ 1 243 426
            - Initial investment cost $ 800 000
            = NPV $ 443 426

3.5.1.2 Internal Rate of Return (IRR) Method

The internal rate of return is the interest rate K at which the present value of expected future cash flows from an investment equals the present value of the cash outlays, so that the NPV = $ 0.

The IRR is calculated by solving for the value of K from the following formula:

$$\frac{FV_1}{(1+K)^1} + \frac{FV_2}{(1+K)^2} + \ldots + \frac{FV_n}{(1+K)^n} - I_0 = 0$$

The IRR can be calculated by trial and error or by computer programs.

If the IRR exceeds the discount rate, also called required rate of return, the investment is profitable and will yield a positive NPV. If the risk of each investment is the same, the higher the IRR, the better. If the IRR and the discount rate are the same, the NPV of the project is zero. If the IRR is less than the discount rate, the NPV of the investment is negative, so that the project is unprofitable and should be rejected.

If the annual cash flows are the same each year, the IRR of the investment is calculated as follows:

Annual cash flow * Discount factor (= appropriate cumulative present value factor for the period in years of the project) − Initial investment cost I_0 = 0

$$\text{Discount factor} = \frac{\text{Initial investment cost } I_0}{\text{Annual cash flow}}$$

When the discount factor has been calculated the figures closest to this value must be found in a table of cumulative present value factors (see Appendix, Table 2), referring to the number of years for which cash flows are received, in order to determine the appropriate IRR.

Example:
Initial investment cost: $ 800 000
Useful life: 3 years
Discount rate: 10 %

Year	Annual cash inflow ($)
1	500 000
2	500 000
3	500 000

The IRR is calculated as follows:

$$\text{Discount factor} = \frac{\text{Initial investment cost } I_0}{\text{Annual cash flow}}$$

$$= \frac{\$\,800\,000}{\$\,500\,000} = 1.6$$

The IRR for this project with a period of 3 years is between 39 % and 40 %, so that the IRR exceeds the discount rate of 10 %. Therefore, this investment should be accepted.

Depreciation is irrelevant in the discounted cash flow analysis (NPV- and IRR method), because the initial investment cost is included as a cash outflow at the beginning of the project, so that deducting depreciation expenses from operating cash inflows would lead to double counting.

3.5.1.3 Comparison of NPV and IRR Method

If there are independent projects with an initial outlay and several cash inflows in later years, the NPV and the IRR method will come to the same result which project should be accepted or rejected. But if there are mutually exclusive projects, where the acceptance of one project excludes the acceptance of another project, it is possible that the NPV and the IRR method lead to different rankings concerning the priority of the projects.

Example:
Discount rate: 10 %

Project	Initial investment cost ($)	Annual cash inflow ($)			NPV method		IRR method	
		Year 1	Year 2	Year 3	$	Rank	%	Rank
I	5 000	3 000	3 000	3 000	2 461	2	36	1
II	20 000	10 000	10 000	10 000	4 869	1	23	2

The IRR method gives an incorrect ranking because
- its results are expressed as a percentage instead in monetary terms, but if a company's objective is to maximize its profit, only the discounted absolute amount of money which an investment yields, measured by the NPV method, is important for quantitative comparisons,

- it is neglected, that if there are no other suitable investments, any surplus funds and interim cash flows due to the acceptance of a project can only be invested at the discount rate, but not at the internal rate of return of this investment.

Therefore, the NPV method is more suitable than the IRR method in making investment decisions.

If a project has negative cash flows in later years, it is possible that as many internal rates of return exist as there are sign changes of the net cash flows, but only one rate of return is economically significant in determining whether the project should be accepted or not.

Example:

Year	Annual cash inflow ($)
0	- 3 000
1	5 000
2	1 000
3	- 3 059

$IRR_1 = 2\%$
$IRR_2 = 36\%$

Discount rate (%)	NPV
< 2 %	negative
2 %	0
> 2 % to < 36 %	positive
36 %	0
> 36 %	negative

The internal rates of return of the project above are 2 % and 36 %. If the IRR of 2 % is used and the discount rate is between 2 % and 36 %, the investment will be incorrectly rejected, although the NPV is positive. Therefore, only the IRR of 36 % will lead to the same decision about the acceptance or rejection of an investment, as if the NPV method were adopted, if the discount rate is higher than 2 %.

3.5.1.4 Modified Internal Rate of Return (MIRR) Method

The deficiency of the IRR method assuming that the annual cash flows are reinvested at the internal rate of return instead of at the cost of capital is overcome by the modified internal rate of return, also called terminal rate of return.

If interest is paid on the net initial investment and the interest rate is the modified internal rate of return, the result equals the terminal value of the cash flows of the investment.

The modified internal rate of return is calculated as follows:

a. Determine the terminal value of the cash flows of the investment by compounding forward all cash flows of the project at the discount rate to the end of the project's life.

b. Calculate the interest rate that, if paid on the net initial investment, will equate this result with the terminal value of the cash flows of the investment:

$$I_0 * (1 + K_m)^n = FV_1 * (1 + K)^{n-1} + FV_2 * (1 + K)^{n-2} + \ldots + FV_n$$

so that

$$K_m = \sqrt[n]{\frac{FV_1 * (1 + K)^{n-1} + FV_2 * (1 + K)^{n-2} + \ldots + FV_n}{I_0}} - 1$$

FV_n = future value of an investment in n years
n = number of years
K = discount rate
K_m = modified internal rate of return
I_0 = initial investment cost, e. g. acquisition cost, invested at the beginning of the project in year 0

If the modified internal rate of return
- exceeds the discount rate, the investment is profitable and will yield a positive NPV. If the risk of each investment is equal, the higher the modified rate of return, the better.
- and the discount rate are equal, the NPV of the project is zero.
- is less than the discount rate, the NPV of the investment is negative, so that the project is unprofitable and should be rejected.

3.5.2 Methods that ignore the Time Value of Money

3.5.2.1 Payback Method

The payback method is also frequently used in practice. Using this method, the length of time is calculated that is required to recover the outlay of an investment by the annual cash inflow of the project.

If an investment has constant cash flows each year (see project I), the payback period is calculated as follows:

$$\text{Payback period} = \frac{\text{Net initial investment}}{\text{Annuity}}$$

If the annual cash flows of an investment are not constant (see project II), the payback period is determined by adding up the expected future cash inflows until the amount of net initial investment of the project is recovered, possibly by using straight-line interpolation.

Managers prefer investments with shorter payback periods to projects with longer payback periods, if all other conditions are equal. Furthermore, projects are accepted if their payback period is within the time limit set by management, ranging mostly from 3 to 5 years.

The major weaknesses of the payback method are:
- it does not discount cash flows and
- the cash flows that an investment yields after the payback period are not taken into account.

Therefore, it can happen that projects are incorrectly ranked by the payback method and, furthermore, investments that have a negative NPV can be accepted by using the payback method (see project III).

Example:

Discount rate: 10 %

Time limit for payback set by management: 3 years

Project	Initial investment cost ($)	Annual cash inflow ($)					
		Year 1	Year 2	Year 3	Year 4	Year 5	Year 6
I	40 000	10 000	10 000	10 000	10 000	10 000	10 000
II	40 000	20 000	20 000	4 000	2 000	1 000	1 000
III	40 000	40 000	1 000	1 000	1 000	1 000	1 000

Project	NPV method			Payback method		
	$	Rank	Project accepted	Payback time (Years)	Rank	Project accepted
I	3 553	1	yes	4	3	no
II	267	2	yes	2	2	yes
III	- 190	3	no	1	1	yes

Using the discounted payback method, all cash flows are first discounted to their present value and the discounted values are then used to determine the payback period of an investment. However, because cash flows that an investment yields after the payback period are not taken into account, it cannot be determined how profitable the project will be.

The payback method is easy to understand and widely used for risky projects in uncertain markets in which it is difficult to predict future cash flows. But because cash flows that an investment yields after the payback period are not taken into account, the payback method should always be used in conjunction with the NPV method, and the cash flows discounted before the payback period is determined.

3.5.2.2 Accounting Rate of Return Method

The accounting rate of return is calculated by the following formula:

$$\text{Accounting rate of return} = \frac{\text{average annual profits}}{\text{average investment}}$$

$$= \frac{\left(\begin{array}{c}\text{incremental revenue} \\ \text{from the project}\end{array} - \begin{array}{c}\text{net investment cost}\end{array}\right) : \begin{array}{c}\text{duration of} \\ \text{the project}\end{array}}{\text{average investment}}$$

The average investment figure used in the denominator of the formula depends on the depreciation method.

For the investments described in 5.2.1 (payback method), the accounting rate of return is calculated as follows, assuming that there are no residual values and straight-line depreciation is used:

Project	Average annual profit ($)	Average investment ($)
I	(60 000 - 40 000) : 6 = 3 333	20 000
II	(48 000 - 40 000) : 6 = 1 333	20 000
III	(45 000 - 40 000) : 6 = 833	20 000

Project	Accounting rate of return	Rank
I	16.67 %	1
II	6.67 %	2
III	4.17 %	3

Usually projects whose accounting rate of return exceeds a required accounting rate of return are accepted - the higher, the better, but projects which still have a positive NPV are sometimes rejected by mistake if its accounting rate of return reduces the overall accounting rate of return.

The accounting rate of return method in which profits instead of cash flows are used is superior to the payback method. The former method considers all profits during the duration of the project and allows differences in the useful life of the assets, whereas the latter neglects the amount of cash inflows that an investment yields after the payback period.

On the other hand, the IRR method is superior to the accounting rate of return method concerning capital investment decisions. Both methods calculate a rate of return percentage, but the latter ignores the time value of money, so that an investment where the cash inflows only occur near the end of its life will have the same accounting rate of return as an investment where the cash inflows occur much earlier, providing that both projects have the same average annual profit and the same average investment. The NPV method, the best method for making capital investment decisions, indicates that the project with the earlier cash inflows is the better one.

Questions and Tasks

1. Blue Company is considering investing in one of three mutually exclusive projects:

	Project A	Project B	Project C
Net initial investment ($)	600 000	450 000	500 000
Residual value ($)	0	0	0
Expected life (years)	4	3	5
Expected cash flow ($):			
Year 1	200 000	250 000	10 000
Year 2	200 000	200 000	90 000
Year 3	200 000	12 000	100 000
Year 4	200 000		300 000
Year 5			250 000

Discount rate: 10 %

Depreciation method: straight-line depreciation

Time limit for payback set by management: 3 years

I. Calculate for each project
a. the net present value,
b. the internal rate of return,
c. the payback period,
d. the accounting rate of return,
e. the modified rate of return.

II. Rank each project according to the capital investment decision methods above.

III. Which project should be accepted according to the capital investment decision methods above?

Enter your results in the following tables:

Project	NPV method			IRR method		
	$	Rank	Project accepted	IRR (%)	Rank	Project accepted
I						
II						
III						

Project	Payback method			Accounting rate of return method		
	Payback time (Years)	Rank	Project accepted	Accounting rate of return (%)	Rank	Project accepted
I						
II						
III						

Project	MIRR method		
	MIRR (%)	Rank	Project accepted
I			
II			
III			

IV. Write a short report to the manager of Blue Company recommending the best of the projects above and give reasons for your recommendation.

V. Determine for project A the constant annual cash flow to achieve
   a. a net present value of $ 97 400.
   b. an internal rate of return of 20 %.

Appendix

Table 1: Discount Factors

Years	Discount rate						
	5 %	8 %	10 %	12 %	15 %	20 %	30 %
1	0.9524	0.9259	0.9091	0.8929	0.8696	0.8333	0.7692
2	0.9070	0.8573	0.8264	0.7972	0.7561	0.6944	0.5917
3	0.8638	0.7938	0.7513	0.7118	0.6575	0.5787	0.4552
4	0.8227	0.7350	0.6830	0.6355	0.5718	0.4823	0.3501
5	0.7835	0.6806	0.6209	0.5674	0.4972	0.4019	0.2693
6	0.7462	0.6302	0.5645	0.5066	0.4323	0.3349	0.2072
7	0.7107	0.5835	0.5132	0.4523	0.3759	0.2791	0.1594
8	0.6768	0.5403	0.4665	0.4039	0.3269	0.2326	0.1226
9	0.6446	0.5002	0.4241	0.3606	0.2843	0.1938	0.0943
10	0.6139	0.4632	0.3855	0.3220	0.2472	0.1615	0.0725

Table 2: Cumulative Discount Factors

Years	Discount rate						
	5 %	8 %	10 %	12 %	15 %	20 %	30 %
1	0.952	0.926	0.909	0.893	0.870	0.833	0.769
2	1.859	1.783	1.736	1.690	1.626	1.528	1.361
3	2.723	2.577	2.487	2.402	2.283	2.106	1.816
4	3.546	3.312	3.170	3.037	2.855	2.589	2.166
5	4.329	3.993	3.791	3.605	3.352	2.991	2.436
6	5.076	4.623	4.355	4.111	3.784	3.326	2.643
7	5.786	5.206	4.868	4.564	4.160	3.605	2.802
8	6.463	5.747	5.335	4.968	4.487	3.837	2.925
9	7.108	6.247	5.759	5.328	4.772	4.031	3.019
10	7.722	6.710	6.145	5.650	5.019	4.192	3.092

Chronological Vocabulary List

Chapter 1: Bookkeeping

1.1 The Balance Sheet

10 bookkeeping — Buchführung
balance sheet — Bilanz
entity — Einheit, Funktionseinheit, juristische Person
liquidation — Liquidation, Liquidierung
assets — Aktivseite der Bilanz
equity and liabilities — Passivseite der Bilanz
liability — Verbindlichkeit
equity — Eigenkapital
total — Bilanzsumme
balance sheet total — Bilanzsumme
acquire — erwerben, erlangen
measurable — messbar
creditor — Gläubiger
claim — Forderung, Anspruch, Anrecht
fund — Vorrat, Geldmittel
paid-in capital — eingezahltes Kapital, Einlagekapital
retained profits — Bilanzgewinn, einbehaltener Gewinn, Gewinnrücklage
retained earnings — Bilanzgewinn, einbehaltener Gewinn, Gewinnrücklage
profit — Ertrag, Gewinn
earnings — Ertrag, Einkommen
omit — weglassen
digit — Ziffer, Dezimalstelle
principle — Grundsatz
regulation — Vorschrift
financial statements — Jahresabschluss
draw up — aufstellen
Generell Accepted Accounting Principles (GAAP) — Grundsätze ordnungsgemäßer Buchführung (GoB)
Commercial Code — Handelsgesetzbuch
principles of preparation — Aufstellungsgrundsätze

11 offsetting prohibited — Saldierungsverbot, Verrechnungsverbot
valuation provisions — Bewertungsvorschriften

	balance sheet continuity	Bilanzidentität, Bilanzkontinuität
	going concern concept	Unternehmensfortführung
	assume	annehmen
	prudence concept	Vorsichtsprinzip
	principle of prudence	Vorsichtsprinzip
	imparity principle	Imparitätsprinzip
	realisation principle	Realisationsprinzip
	accruals concept	Periodenabgrenzung
	matching principle	Periodenabgrenzung
	income	Ertrag, Einkommen
	expense	Aufwand
	consistency concept	Bewertungsstetigkeit
	historical cost principle	Anschaffungskostenprinzip
	cost	Kosten
	state	darlegen, aussagen, festsetzen
	purchase	Einkauf, Kauf
	depreciation	Abschreibung
	redemption	Ablösung, Tilgung, Rückzahlung
12	corporation	Kapitalgesellschaft
	notes (to the financial statements)	Anhang (zum Jahresabschluss)
	in compliance with	in Übereinstimmung mit
	a true and fair view	ein den tatsächlichen Verhältnissen entsprechendes Bild
	financial position	Finanzlage
	explanatory	erklärend, erläuternd
	prescribe	vorschreiben
	heading	Posten
	extent	Umfang
	management report	Lagebericht
	annual report	Geschäftsbericht
	contents	Inhalt
	derive	ableiten
	ordiance	Verordnung
	preparation	Aufstellung, Vorbereitung
	audit	Buchprüfung
	disclosure	Offenlegung, Bekanntmachung
	size classifications	Größenklassen
	medium-sized	mittelgroß
13	current assets	Umlaufvermögen
	inventories	Vorräte

	accounts receivable	Forderungen
	securities	Wertpapiere
	prepaid expenses	Rechnungsabgrenzungsposten der Aktivseite
	intangible	unberührbar, immateriell
	disclose	bekannt machen, mitteilen
	balance sheet date	Bilanzstichtag
	expenditure	Ausgabe
	fixed assets	Anlagevermögen
	trademark	Schutzmarke, Warenzeichen
	patent	Patent
	goodwill	Geschäfts- oder Firmenwert
	tangible assets	Sachanlagen
	subtract	abziehen, subtrahieren
	accumulate	anhäufen, ansammeln
	depreciation	Abschreibung
	current liabilities	kurzfristige Verbindlichkeiten
	long-term liabilities	langfristige Verbindlichkeiten
	accrued liabilities	Rückstellungen
	accruals	Rückstellungen
	defer	hinausschieben, verschieben
	deferred income	Rechnungsabgrenzungsposten der Passivseite
14	receipt	Einnahme
	subscribed capital	gezeichnetes Kapital
	capital reserves	Kapitalrücklage
	earnings reserves	Gewinnrücklage
	retain	zurückbehalten, einbehalten
	retained earnings brought forward	Gewinnvortrag
	accumulated losses brought forward	Verlustvortrag
	net income for the year	Jahresüberschuss
	net loss for the year	Jahresfehlbetrag

1.2 Different Balance Sheet Changes

16	transaction	Transaktion
	record	aufzeichnen, eintragen, registrieren
	book	buchen
	entry	Buchung
	enter	buchen
	double-entry system	System der doppelten Buchführung
	T-account	T-Konto

	asset accounts	aktive Bestandskonten
	opening balance sheet	Eröffnungsbilanz
	closing balance sheet	Schlussbilanz
	beginning balance	Anfangsbestand
	opening balance	Anfangsbestand
	increase	zunehmen, sich vergrößern, wachsen
	decrease	abnehmen, sich vermindern
	liability and equity accounts	passive Bestandskonten
	balance	Saldo, Restbestand, Schlussbestand
	debit	Soll
	credit	Haben
	debit an account	eine Sollbuchung vornehmen
17	credit an account	eine Habenbuchung vornehmen
	debit balance	Sollsaldo
	credit balance	Habensaldo
	equal	gleichen, gleich sein, ergeben
	sale	Verkauf
	merchandise	Handelswaren
	income statement	Gewinn- und Verlustrechnung
	profit and loss statement	Gewinn- und Verlustrechnung
	closing entry	Abschlussbuchung
	income summary	Gewinn- und Verlustkonto
	profit and loss account	Gewinn- und Verlustkonto
18	withdrawal	Abhebung, Entnahme
	withdraw	abheben, entnehmen
	ledger	Hauptbuch
	journal	Grundbuch
	book of original	Grundbuch
	journal entry	Grundbucheintragung
	original entry	Grundbucheintragung
	prime entry	Grundbucheintragung
	entry	Buchung
	posting	Buchung
	post	buchen
19	ledger sheet	Kontenblatt

1.3 Revenues and Expenses

20	accounting period	Abrechnungszeitraum
	fiscal year	Abrechnungsjahr, Geschäftsjahr
	cash receipt	Geldeingang, Kasseneinnahme

	advance	Vorschuss
	advance payments	Vorauszahlung
21	bad debt	uneinbringliche Forderung
	write off	abschreiben
	allowance for doubtful accounts	Wertberichtigung auf Forderungen
	depreciation	Abschreibung
	depreciate	abschreiben
22	provision	Rückstellung
	provision for income taxes	Aufwand für Ertragsteuer

1.4 Inventory and Different Methods of its Valuation for the Calculation of the Cost of Sales

23	calculate	kalkulieren, berechnen
	cost of sales	Anschaffungs- und Herstellkosten der verkauften Ware, Wareneinsatz, Selbstkosten, Umsatzkosten
	sales revenues	Umsatzerlöse für Waren
	perpetual inventory taking	permanente Inventur
	physical inventory taking	Inventur durch körperliche Bestandsaufnahme
	spoil	vernichten, zerstören, beschädigen
	shrinkage	Schwund, Wertverlust, Verminderung
24	assign	festlegen, festsetzen, bestimmen
25	overheads, overhead costs	Gemeinkosten
	costs	Kosten
	overhead expenses	Gemeinkosten
	expenses	Kosten, Aufwendungen
	incur	auf sich nehmen

1.5 Depreciation Methods for Noncurrent Assets

27	capital lease	Leasing
	lessee	Leasingnehmer
	lessor	Leasinggeber
	acquisition	Erwerb, Anschaffung
	acquisition costs	Anschaffungskosten, Einstandskosten
	service life	Nutzungsdauer
	useful life	(technische) Lebensdauer
	depreciation	Abschreibung
	depreciation expense	Abschreibungsaufwand
	wear out	abnutzen, verbrauchen
	obsolete	veraltet

	residual value	Restwert
	depreciable cost	abschreibbare Kosten eines Gutes des Anlagevermögens
	depreciation method	Abschreibungsmethode
	unit-of-production depreciation method	Abschreibungsmethode nach Produktionseinheiten
28	straight-line depreciation	lineare Abschreibung
	percentage	Prozentsatz
	depreciation rate	Abschreibungsrate, Prozentsatz der Abschreibung
	accelerated depreciation	Sonderabschreibung, die über die normale Abschreibung hinausgeht
	accumulated depreciation	aufgelaufene Abschreibungen
	book value	Buchwert
29	depreciate, write off	abschreiben
	gain on sale	Veräußerungsgewinn
	loss on sale	Veräußerungsverlust
	Internal Revenue Service (IRS)	Finanzbehörde (USA)
	deferred income tax	Einkommensteuerverbindlichkeit, Steuerstundung
	wasting asset	kurzfristig abnutzbares Wirtschaftsgut
	timber	Holzbestand, Baumbestand
	depletion	Abschreibung von Bodenschätzen (Substanzverzehr)
	deplete	Bodenschätze abschreiben
	depletion expense	Aufwand für Substanzverzehr, z. B. Abbau von Bodenschätzen
	amortization	Abschreibung auf immaterielle Vermögenswerte

1.6 Equity and Liabilities

31	sole proprietorship	Einzelunternehmen
	sole proprietor, sole trader	Einzelkaufmann
	proprietor	Inhaber
	partnership	Personengesellschaft
	general partnership	offene Handelsgesellschaft, OHG
	limited partnership	Kommanditgesellschaft, KG
	partner	Gesellschafter
	general partner	Komplementär, Vollhafter
	limited partner	Kommanditist, Teilhafter

	corporation	Kapitalgesellschaft
	public limited company	Aktiengesellschaft, AG
	share, stock	Aktie
	shareholder, stockholder	Aktionär, Anteilseigner
	common stockholder	Stammaktionär
	common stock	Stammaktie
	preferred stockholder	Vorzugsaktionär
	preferred stock	Vorzugsaktie
	treasury stock	eigene Aktien
32	dividend	Dividende
	stock dividend	Gratisaktie
	working capital	kurzfristiges Betriebskapital (= Umlaufvermögen abzüglich der kurzfristigen Verbindlichkeiten)
	debt capital	Fremdkapital (langfristig)
	permanent capital	Eigenkapital + Fremdkapital (langfristig)
	issuance	Ausgabe
	bond	Bond, Schuldverschreibung, Anleihe
	due date	Fälligkeitstag
	issuer	Aussteller, Ausgeber
	principal	Kapital
	zero-coupon bond	Nullcouponanleihe, abgezinste Anleihe
33	the former	der/die/das Erstere, erstere(r, s)
	the latter	der/die/das Letztere, letztere(r, s)
	parent company	Muttergesellschaft, Konzernobergesellschaft
	subsidiary (company)	Tochtergesellschaft
	annual financial statements	Jahresabschluss
	consolidated financial statements	Konzernabschluss
	intercompany transactions	Konzerngeschäftsvorfälle, Geschäfte zwischen verbundenen Unternehmen
	consolidated profit and loss account	Konzern-Gewinn- und Verlustrechnung
	consolidated income statement	Konzern-Gewinn- und Verlustrechnung
	consolidated retained earnings	Konzerngewinn
	consolidated balance sheet	Konzernbilanz, konsolidierte Bilanz
	group	Konzern

1.7 What is a Cash Flow Statement?

35	cash flow statement	Kapitalflussrechnung
	cash flow	Kapitalfluss, Cash Flow

	profitability	Rentabilität
	liquidity	Liquidität
	US-GAAP (= Generell Accepted Accounting Principles)	GoB (= Grundsätze ordnungsgemäßer Buchführung)
36	adjustment	Berichtigung
37	redemption	Rückkauf
38	investment	Investition
40	accounts payable	Verbindlichkeiten

1.8 Ratios

42	auditing	Prüfungswesen, Rechnungsprüfung, Wirtschaftsprüfung
	examination	Prüfung
	auditor	Wirtschaftsprüfer, Betriebsprüfer
	company's annual report	Geschäftsbericht eines Unternehmens
	numerator	Zähler
	denominator	Nenner
	ability	Fähigkeit
	current ratio	Liquiditätskennzahl (Umlaufvermögen : kurzfrist. Verbindlichk.)
	ratio	Verhältnis, Quotient
	liquidity	Liquidität, Zahlungsfähigkeit
43	receivables	Forderungen, Außenstände
	inventory turnover ratio	Lagerumschlagshäufigkeit
	tie up capital	Kapital binden, Kapital festlegen
	obsolete	veraltet, altmodisch
	competitor	Mitbewerber, Konkurrent
	debt ratio	Verschuldungsgrad
	solvency	Solvenz, Zahlungsfähigkeit, Fähigkeit zur Bezahlung langfristiger Verbindlichkeiten
44	highly leveraged	stark fremdkapitalfinanziert
	return on equity (ROE)	Eigenkapitalrendite, Eigenkapitalrentabilität
45	gross (profit) margin	Bruttogewinnspanne
	profit margin	Gewinnspanne
	earnings per share	Ergebnis pro Aktie
46	price-earnings ratio	Kurs-Gewinn-Verhältnis
	return on investment (ROI)	Kapitalverzinsung
	profitability	Rentabilität
47	capital turnover	Kapitalumschlag

Chapter 2: Cost Accounting

2.1 Introduction

51
cost accounting	Kostenrechnung
plan	Plan
variance	Abweichung
internal	intern
cost per unit	Stückkosten
unit cost	Stückkosten
average cost	Durchschnittskosten
rate	bewerten, bemessen
output	Leistung, Ertrag, Ausstoß, Produktionsmenge
fixed costs	Fixkosten, fixe Kosten
relate	verbinden, verknüpfen, sich beziehen
depreciation	Abschreibung
insurance premium	Versicherungsbeitrag
variable costs	variable Kosten
piecework	Akkordarbeit
direct material	Fertigungsmaterial, Produktionsmaterial
direct costs	Einzelkosten
indirect costs	Gemeinkosten
overheads	Gemeinkosten
voucher	Beleg
special direct costs	Sondereinzelkosten
special direct sales costs	Sondereinzelkosten des Vertriebs
special direct costs of sales	Sondereinzelkosten des Vertriebs
special direct manufacturing costs	Sondereinzelkosten der Fertigung
special direct costs of production	Sondereinzelkosten der Fertigung
assign	zuweisen, zuteilen
product costing scheme	Kalkulationsschema

52
unit of cost	Kostenträger
cost center	Kostenstelle
cost distribution sheet	Betriebsabrechnungsbogen
cost center accounting	Kostenstellenrechnung

2.2 Cost Element Accounting

cost element accounting	Kostenartenrechnung
cost type accounting	Kostenartenrechnung
cost elements	Kostenarten
cost types	Kostenarten

	personnel costs	Personalkosten
	overtime payment	Überstundenvergütung
	social security contributions	Sozialversicherungsbeiträge
	voluntary employee benefit expenses	freiwillige soziale Aufwendungen
	severance payment	Abfindung
	time-rate wage	Zeitlohn
	incentive wage	Leistungslohn
	piecework	Akkordarbeit
	imputed entrepreneurial salary	kalkulatorischer Unternehmerlohn
	partnership	Personengesellschaft
	sole proprietorship	Einzelunternehmen
	general partnership	offene Handelsgesellschaft, OHG
	limited partnership	Kommanditgesellschaft, KG
53	general manager	Geschäftsführer
	managing partner	geschäftsführender Gesellschafter
	corporation	Kapitalgesellschaft
	limited (liability) company	Gesellschaft mit beschränkter Haftung, GmbH
	private limited company	Gesellschaft mit beschränkter Haftung, GmbH
	public stock corporation	Aktiengesellschaft, AG
	public (limited) company	Aktiengesellschaft, AG
	material costs	Materialkosten
	raw material	Rohstoff
	operating supplies	Betriebsstoffe
	manufacturing supplies	Hilfs- und Betriebsstoffe
	inventory method	Inventurmethode
	impute	zuschreiben, beimessen, anrechnen
	imputed depreciation	kalkulatorische Abschreibung
	wear and tear	Verschleiß
	residual value	Restwert
	unit-of-production depreciation	Leistungsabschreibung, stückbezogene Abschreibung
	straight-line depreciation	lineare Abschreibung
	declining-balance method of depreciation	degressive Abschreibung
	sum-of-the-years-digits method of depreciation	digitale Abschreibung, arithmetisch-degressive Abschreibung
	manufacturing assets	Produktionsmittel
	write off	abschreiben
	replacement cost	Wiederbeschaffungskosten

	current market value	Tageswert
	acquisition cost	Anschaffungskosten
	cost of goods manufactured	Herstellungskosten
	service life	Nutzungsdauer
	useful life	Nutzungsdauer
	accounting	Rechnungswesen
	depreciation for tax purposes	steuerliche Abschreibungen
	costing	Kostenermittlung
	balance sheet depreciation	buchmäßige Abschreibung
	cost of sales accounting method	Umsatzkostenverfahren
54	imputed interest	kalkulatorische Zinsen
	imputed costs	kalkulatorische Kosten
	opportunity costs	Opportunitätskosten
	imputed risk costs	kalkulatorische Wagniskosten
	storage	Lagerung
	outside services	Fremdleistungen
	utilities	Energieversorgungsbetriebe
	lease	Pacht
	consulting	Beratung
	hospitality	Bewirtung, Gastlichkeit

2.3 Cost Center Accounting

55	cost center accounting	Kostenstellenrechnung
	allocation rate	Verrechnungssatz, Zuschlagssatz
	product costing	Kostenträgerstückrechnung
	activity unit	Bezugsgröße
	manufacturing cost center	Fertigungskostenstelle
	issue of material	Materialausgabe
	raw material warehouse	Materiallager
	cost distribution sheet	Betriebsabrechnungsbogen
56	internal cost allocation	innerbetriebliche Leistungsverrechnung
	intracompany services charging	innerbetriebliche Leistungsverrechnung
	intracompany	innerbetrieblich
	intracompany services	innerbetriebliche Leistungen
	internal services	innerbetriebliche Leistungen
	internal transfer price	innerbetrieblicher Verrechnungspreis
	transfer price	Verrechnungspreis
	comply with the law	sich an die Gesetze halten
	operating department	Fachabteilung
	production department	Produktionsabteilung

	support department	Nebenkostenstelle
	service department	Nebenkostenstelle
	reciprocal	gegenseitig, wechselseitig
57	direct allocation method	Anbauverfahren
	direct method	Anbauverfahren
	own use	Eigenverbrauch
59	step-down allocation method	Stufenleiterverfahren, Treppenverfahren
	sequential allocation method	Stufenleiterverfahren, Treppenverfahren
	partial	partiell, teilweise
	render	leisten, übergeben, unterbreiten
	rank	einreihen, einordnen, klassifizieren
	order	Ordnung, Anordnung, Reihenfolge, Folge
	proceed	fortsetzen, weitermachen
	sequence	Reihenfolge, Anordnung, Folge
60	subsequent	nachfolgend, folgend
61	reciprocal allocation method	simultane Leistungsverrechnung, Kostenstellenausgleichsverfahren
	accurate	genau
	reciprocate	austauschen, wechseln

2.4 Product Cost Accounting

65	product cost accounting	Kostenträgerrechnung
	product costing	Kostenträgerstückrechnung
	cost object	Kostenträger
	cost of production	Herstellkosten
	cost price	Selbstkosten
	unit price	Stückpreis
	profit per unit	Stückgewinn
	product costing scheme	Kalkulationsschema der Kostenträgerrechnung
	activity unit	Bezugsgröße
	allocation rate	Gemeinkostenverrechnungssatz
	burden rate	Gemeinkostensatz
	process cost system	Divisions(-stufen)kalkulation
	overhead percentage cost calculation	Zuschlagskalkulation
	overhead rate	Gemeinkostensatz (als Zuschlagssatz)
	material cost overhead rate	Materialgemeinkostenzuschlag
	material handling charge	Materialgemeinkostenzuschlag
	manufacturing overhead rate	Fertigungsgemeinkostenzuschlag
	apportionment of indirect cost	Gemeinkostenumlage

	special direct costs	Sondereinzelkosten
66	joint production process	Kuppelproduktion
	joint	gemeinschaftlich
	joint product	Kuppelprodukt
	main product	Hauptprodukt
	by-product	Nebenprodukt
	split-off point	Trennpunkt der Produktion, Zeitpunkt der getrennten Fertigung
	trace	zurückverfolgen, zurückführen
	cost	kalkulieren, kosten
71	premature	vorzeitig
72	scrap	Schrott
	waste	Abfall
	rectify	berichtigen, verbessern
	rectification	Berichtigung
	product costing per period	Kostenträgerzeitrechnung
	period costing	Kostenträgerzeitrechnung
	operating result	Betriebsergebnis
	period accounting method	Gesamtkostenverfahren
73	cost of sales method	Umsatzkostenverfahren

2.5 Cost-Volume-Profit (CVP) Analysis

74	cost driver	Kostentreiber
	monopoly	Monopol
	curvilinear	krummlinig, gekrümmt
	outweigh	übertreffen
75	steep	steil
	bottleneck	Engpass, Flaschenhals
	step cost function	abschnittsweise definierte Kostenfunktion, Kostenfunktion in Form einer Treppenfunktion
	marginal revenue	Grenzerlös
	marginal costs	Grenzkosten
	break-even point	Gewinnschwelle
	polypoly	Polypol
76	capacity	Kapazität
	contribution margin	Deckungsbeitrag
	contribution margin per unit	Deckungsbeitrag pro Stück
79	impact	Einfluss, (Aus-)Wirkung

2.6 What is the Difference between Variable Costing and Absorption Costing?

82	variable costing	Teilkostenrechnung
	absorption costing	Vollkostenrechnung
	direct costing	Teilkostenrechnung
	marginal costing	Teilkostenrechnung
	assign	zuweisen, zuteilen
	manufacturing cost	Herstellkosten
	include	enthalten, einbeziehen
	incur	auf sich laden, auf sich nehmen
	direct costs	Einzelkosten, direkte Kosten
	marginal costs	Grenzkosten
	full costing	Vollkostenrechnung
83	budget	im Haushaltsplan vorsehen, planen
84	income statement	Gewinn- und Verlustrechnung, Ergebnisrechnung
	contribution margin	Deckungsbeitrag
	operating income	Betriebsgewinn
85	adjustment	Anpassung, Angleichung
	overheads	Gemeinkosten, indirekte Kosten
	gross margin	Bruttogewinn, Rohertrag
86	lump sum	Pauschalbetrag
88	storing charges	Lagerkosten
	charges	Kosten
90	deliberately	vorsätzlich, absichtlich
	significant	bedeutsam
	distort	verzerren, verdrehen
91	absorb	aufnehmen, absorbieren
	defer	verzögern
	maintenance	Wartung, Instandhaltung
	overvalued	überbewertet
	surplus	Überschuss
	dispose of	beseitigen, verkaufen, loswerden
92	actual costs	Istkosten
	voucher	Beleg
	standard costing	Standardkostenrechnung, Plankostenrechnung
	flexible budget	Sollkosten
	planned costs	Plankosten
93	actual activity	Istleistung
	variance	Abweichung

	variance analysis	Abweichungsanalyse
	comparison of budget with actual figures	Soll-Ist-Vergleich
	utilization	Verwendung, Anwendung, Inanspruchnahme
94	downward demand spiral	abwärtsgerichtete Nachfragespirale, spiralförmig abnehmende Nachfrage
95	stepwise contribution accounting	stufenweise Deckungsbeitragsrechnung
	activity unit	Bezugsgröße
	linear programming	lineare Programmierung
	contribution margin steps	Deckungsbeitragsstufen
	structure costs	Strukturkosten (Fixkosten)
	structure costs of the product	Produktstrukturkosten, Erzeugnisfixkosten
	structure costs of the product group	Produktgruppenstrukturkosten, Erzeugnisgruppenfixkosten
	sales structure costs	Verkaufsstrukturkosten
96	administration structure costs	Verwaltungsstrukturkosten
	product contribution	Produktdeckungsbeitrag
	product group contribution	Produktgruppendeckungsbeitrag
	liquidity-related contribution	liquiditätswirksamer Deckungsbeitrag
97	excessive	übermäßig
	buildup	Aufbau

Chapter 3: Economics

3.1 Vocational School, Apprenticeship and Banking

99

economics	Wirtschaftslehre, Volkswirtschaftslehre, Wirtschaftswissenschaft
vocational school	Berufsschule
apprenticeship	Ausbildung(-sverhältnis), Lehre
catering	Gastronomie
probationary period	Probezeit
trial period	Probezeit
dismiss	entlassen
without notice	fristlos
notice	Kündigung
protection against dismissal	Kündigungsschutz
dismissal	Entlassung
give notice	kündigen
oral	mündlich
verbal	mündlich
resident's registration office	Einwohnermeldeamt
application form	Antragsformular
syllable	Silbe
widowed	verwitwet
divorced	geschieden
specimen signature	Unterschriftsprobe
joint account	Gemeinschaftskonto
account	Konto
account holder	Kontoinhaber
standing order	Dauerauftrag
overdraft	Kontoüberziehung, Überziehungskredit
overdraft facility	Dispositionskredit
overdraw	überziehen (Konto)
survey	Untersuchung, Analyse, Überblick
outstanding	hervorragend
value for money	Preis-Leistungs-Verhältnis
wear and tear	Abnutzung, Verschleiß
depreciation	Abschreibung
subsidiary	Tochterunternehmen
pan-European	gesamteuropäisch
subsidize	subventionieren

	General Business Conditions	allgemeine Geschäftsbedingungen
	the small print	das Kleingedruckte
	sales contract	Kaufvertrag
100	installment	Rate
	handling charge	Bearbeitungsgebühr
	payment on open account	Zahlung gegen Rechnung (mit offenem Zahlungsziel)
	default	Zahlungsverzug
	default	in Zahlungsverzug geraten
	deferred payment	Stundung der Zahlung
	pledge	Pfand
	pledge	verpfänden
	reminder	Mahnung
	statement of account	Kontoauszug
	bank statement	Kontoauszug
	statement printer	Kontoauszugsdrucker
	magnetic strip	Magnetstreifen
	account balance	Kontostand
	be in the red	in den roten Zahlen sein
	withdrawal	Abhebung
	seize	pfänden
	seizure	Pfändung
	auction off	versteigern
	debit	Abbuchung
	debit	abbuchen, belasten
	note	Geldschein
	European Central Bank (ECB)	Europäische Zentralbank
	tamper-proof	fälschungssicher
	forge	fälschen, nachmachen
	purchasing power	Kaufkraft
	currency	Währung
	stable	stabil
	tax bracket	Steuerklasse
	declare	versteuern
	percentage	Prozentsatz
	gross	brutto
	net	netto
101	expiry date	Verfallsdatum
	compensation	Schadenersatz, Entschädigung
	seasonal sale	Schlussverkauf

	share	Aktie, Anteil, Geschäftsanteil
	IPO (initial public offering)	Börsengang
	float a company	ein Unternehmen an die Börse bringen
	flotation	Börsengang
	launch something onto the market	etwas auf den Markt bringen
	fluctuation	Schwankung
	mail order business	Versandunternehmen
	fluctuate	schwanken
	glut	Übermaß, Überangebot
	sift the wheat from the chaff	die Spreu vom Weizen trennen
	free of charge	kostenlos
	portfolio	Portefeuille, Bestand, Depot
	self-employed	selbstständig
	entrepreneur	Unternehmer
	GDP (gross domestic product)	Bruttoinlandsprodukt (BIP)
	domestic	inländisch
	GNP (gross national product)	Bruttosozialprodukt (BSP)
	operating costs	Betriebskosten
	competition	Konkurrenz, Wettbewerb
	competitive	wettbewerbsfähig, konkurrenzfähig
	competitor	Wettbewerber
	real estate	Immobilien
	grant	gewähren, bewilligen
	grace period	Zahlungsfrist
	at your disposal	zur Verfügung
102	basic data	Eckdaten
	customer's reference number	Kundennummer
	German bank's credit reference agency	SCHUFA
	register	eintragen
	land-charge	Grundschuld
	guarantee	Bürgschaft
	guarantor	Bürge, Garant
	repayment	Tilgung, Zurückzahlung
	pay off	tilgen, zurückzahlen
	pay back	zurückzahlen
	repay	tilgen, zurückzahlen
	statute	Satzung
	interest rate	Zinssatz

APR (annual percentage rate)	Jahreszins
true APR	effektiver Jahreszins
monetary policy (Friedman)	Geldpolitik, Monetarismus
fiscal policy (Keynesianism)	Fiskalpolitik, Keynesianismus
tangible assets	Sachanlagevermögen
intangible assets	immaterielle(-s) Vermögen(-swerte)
economy of scale	Kostendegression
free-market ideology	Idee der freien Markwirtschaft
data privacy	Datenschutz
data protection	Datenschutz
money laundering	Geldwäsche
report	Bericht, Reportage, (Schul-)Zeugnis

103
personal status	Familienstand
weigh up the pros and cons	das Für und Wider abwägen
direct debit	Abbuchungs-, Einzugsverfahren, Lastschrift
direct debit authorization	Einzugsermächtigung
means of payment	Zahlungsmittel
method of payment	Zahlungsweise
line of business	Branche
govern	regeln
in advance	im Voraus
pay in cash	bar bezahlen
pay in	einzahlen
forgery	Banknotenfälschung

104
stocks	Aktien, Lager(-bestand)
stock exchange	Börse
issue	ausgeben, emittieren
price range	Preisspanne
articles of association	Gesellschaftssatzung, Gesellschaftsvertrag
location factor	Standortfaktor
receivable	Forderung
expire under statute of limitations	verjähren
statutory limitation period	Verjährungsfrist
statute of limitation	Verjährung

3.2 Quantitative Models for the Planning, Management and Control of Stocks

105	economic order quantity (EOQ)	optimale Bestellmenge
	tie	festlegen (Geld), binden
	be spoiled	schlecht werden
	consider	betrachten, erwägen, berücksichtigen
	replenish	wieder auffüllen, ergänzen, vervollständigen
	re-order point	Meldebestand
	bin card	Lagerfachkarte, Lagerbestandskarte
	requisition	Anforderung
106	purchase movements card	Einkaufspendelkarte
	purchasing department	Einkaufsabteilung
	purchase stock card	Einkaufsstammkarte
	stores department	Lagerabteilung
	accounts department	Rechnungswesen (Abteilung)
	holding costs	Lager(-haltungs)kosten
	ordering costs	Bestellkosten
	increment	Wachstum, Zuwachs, Zunahme
	obsolescence	Veralterung
	deterioration	Verschlechterung, (Wert-)Minderung, Verderb
107	clerical costs	Schreibkosten, Bürokosten
	irrespective of	unabhängig von
	base stock, safety stock	eiserner Bestand, Mindestlagerbestand
	stock	Lagerbestand
108	average stock	durchschnittlicher Lagerbestand
111	balance	abwägen, wiegen
	batch	Stapel, Ladung
112	re-order point	Meldebestand
	lead time	Lieferzeit
	elapse	vergehen, verfließen, verstreichen
	base stock, safety stock	eiserner Bestand, Mindestbestand
	uncertainty	Unsicherheit
	idle time	Stillstandszeit, Leerlaufzeit, Wartezeit
	maximum stock	Höchstbestand
113	turnover rate	Umschlagshäufigkeit
	average time of storage	durchschnittliche Lagerdauer
114	ABC classification method	ABC-Analyse
	elaborate	sorgfältig ausgearbeitet
	consistent with	in Übereinstimmung mit, im Einklang mit
	sophisticated	hoch entwickelt, verfeinert

3.3 Benchmaking
118	benchmarking	Benchmarking, Leistungsvergleich, Vergleich des eigenen Unternehmens mit den besten Konkurrenten und den besten brachenfremden Unternehmen
	compete	im Wettbewerb stehen, konkurrieren, sich messen
	line of business	Branche
	benchmark	Bezugswert, Maßstab

3.4 Office Equipment

adhesive tape	Klebeband
calculator	Taschenrechner
carbon paper	Kohlepapier
cartridge	Tintenpatrone
date stamp	Datumsstempel
drawing pin	Heftzwecke
envelope	(Brief-)Umschlag
file	Akte
filing cabinet	Aktenschrank
folder	Schnellhefter, Aktendeckel, Mappe
fountain pen	Füller, Füllfederhalter
glue	Klebstoff
guillotine	Papierschneidemaschine
ink-pad	Stempelkissen
(pair of) compasses	Zirkel
(pair of) scissors	Schere
paper clip	Büroklammer
pencil sharpener	Bleistiftanspitzer
pointer	Zeigestock
punch	Locher
rubber (B. E.)	Radiergummi
eraser (A. E.)	Radiergummi
ruler	Lineal
staple	Heftklammer
stapler	Heftmaschine
transparency	Folie
typewriter	Schreibmaschine

3.5 Capital Investment Decisions

120	investment	Investition, Geldanlage, Kapitalanlage
	elapse	vergehen, verfließen, verstreichen
	outlay	(Geld-)Ausgabe
	acquisition cost	Anschaffungskosten
	recoupment	Wiedereinbringung von Verlusten, Ausgaben etc.
	commitment	Bindung
	funds	Mittel
	discount rate	Abzinsungssatz
121	net present value	Kapitalwert
	present value	Barwert, Gegenwartswert
	net present value method	Kapitalwertmethode
	NPV method	Kapitalwertmethode
	reject	ablehnen
122	annuity	Annuität, Rente, (jährlich) identische Beträge
123	internal rate of return	interner Zinssatz
	internal rate of return method	interne Zinssatz Methode
	IRR method	interne Zinssatz Methode
124	rate of return	Kapitalverzinsung, Rendite
127	modified rate of return	kritischer Sollzinssatz
	terminal rate of return	kritischer Sollzinssatz
	pay interest (on)	verzinsen
	terminal value	(Vermögens-) Endwert
129	payback method	statische Amortisationsrechnung
	payback period	Amortisationszeit
130	discounted payback method	dynamische Amortisationsrechnung
131	accounting rate of return method	Rentabilitätsvergleichsrechnung
132	duration	Dauer

Alphabetical Vocabulary List (English – German)

a true and fair view 12	ein den tatsächlichen Verhältnissen entsprechendes Bild
ABC classification method 114	ABC-Analyse
ability 42	Fähigkeit
absorb 91	aufnehmen, absorbieren
absorption costing 82	Vollkostenrechnung
accelerated depreciation 28	Sonderabschreibung, die über die normale Abschreibung hinausgeht
account 99	Konto
account balance 100	Kontostand
account holder 99	Kontoinhaber
accounting 53	Rechnungswesen
accounting period 20	Abrechnungszeitraum
accounting rate of return method 131	Rentabilitätsvergleichsrechnung
accounts department 106	Rechnungswesen (Abteilung)
accounts payable 40	Verbindlichkeiten
accounts receivable 13	Forderungen
accruals 13	Rückstellungen
accruals concept 11	Periodenabgrenzung
accrued liabilities 13	Rückstellungen
accumulate 13	anhäufen, ansammeln
accumulated depreciation 28	aufgelaufene Abschreibungen
accumulated losses brought forward 14	Verlustvortrag
accurate 61	genau
acquire 10	erwerben, erlangen
acquisition 27	Erwerb, Anschaffung
acquisition costs 27, 53, 120	Anschaffungskosten, Einstandskosten
activity unit 55, 65, 99	Bezugsgröße
actual activity 93	Istleistung
actual costs 92	Istkosten
adhesive tape 118	Klebeband

adjustment 36, 85	Berichtigung, Anpassung, Angleichung
administration structure costs 96	Verwaltungsstrukturkosten
advance 20	Vorschuss
advance payments 20	Vorauszahlung
allocation rate 55	Verrechnungssatz, Zuschlagssatz
allocation rate 65	Gemeinkostenverrechnungssatz
allowance for doubtful accounts 21	Wertberichtigung auf Forderungen
amortization 29	Abschreibung auf immaterielle Vermögenswerte
annual financial statements 33	Jahresabschluss
annual percentage rate (APR) 102	Jahreszins
annual report 12	Geschäftsbericht
annuity 122	Annuität, Rente, (jährlich) identische Beträge
application form 99	Antragsformular
apportionment of indirect cost 65	Gemeinkostenumlage
apprenticeship 99	Ausbildung(-sverhältnis), Lehre
APR (annual percentage rate) 102	Jahreszins
articles of association 104	Gesellschaftssatzung, Gesellschaftsvertrag
asset accounts 16	aktive Bestandskonten
assets 10	Aktivseite der Bilanz
assign 24	festlegen, festsetzen, bestimmen
assign 51, 82	zuweisen, zuteilen
assume 11	annehmen
at your disposal 101	zur Verfügung
auction off 100	versteigern
audit 12	Buchprüfung
auditing 42	Prüfungswesen, Rechnungsprüfung, Wirtschaftsprüfung
auditor 42	Wirtschaftsprüfer, Betriebsprüfer
average cost 51	Durchschnittskosten
average stock 108	durchschnittlicher Lagerbestand
average time of storage 113	durchschnittliche Lagerdauer
bad debt 21	uneinbringliche Forderung
balance 111	abwägen, wiegen
balance 16	Saldo, Restbestand, Schlussbestand

balance sheet 10	Bilanz
balance sheet continuity 11	Bilanzidentität, Bilanzkontinuität
balance sheet date 13	Bilanzstichtag
balance sheet depreciation 53	buchmäßige Abschreibung
balance sheet total 10	Bilanzsumme
bank statement 100	Kontoauszug
base stock 107, 112	eiserner Bestand, Mindestbestand
basic data 102	Eckdaten
batch 111	Stapel, Ladung
be in the red 100	in den roten Zahlen sein
be spoiled 105	schlecht werden
beginning balance 16	Anfangsbestand
benchmark 118	Bezugswert, Maßstab
benchmarking 118	Benchmarking, Leistungsvergleich, Vergleich des eigenen Unternehmens mit den besten Konkurrenten und den besten branchenfremden Unternehmen
bin card 105	Lagerfachkarte, Lagerbestandskarte
bond 32	Bond, Schuldverschreibung, Anleihe
book 16	buchen
book of original 18	Grundbuch
book value 28	Buchwert
bookkeeping 10	Buchführung
bottleneck 75	Engpass, Flaschenhals
break-even point 75	Gewinnschwelle
budget 83	im Haushaltsplan vorsehen, planen
buildup 97	Aufbau
burden rate 65	Gemeinkostensatz
business administration 3	Betriebswirtschaftslehre
by-product 66	Nebenprodukt
calculate 23	kalkulieren, berechnen
calculator 118	Taschenrechner
capacity 76	Kapazität
capital lease 27	Leasing
capital reserves 14	Kapitalrücklage
capital turnover 47	Kapitalumschlag

carbon paper 118	Kohlepapier
cartridge 118	Tintenpatrone
cash flow 35	Kapitalfluss, Cash Flow
cash flow statement 35	Kapitalflussrechnung
cash receipt 20	Geldeingang, Kasseneinnahme
catering 99	Gastronomie
charges 88	Kosten
claim 10	Forderung, Anspruch, Anrecht
clerical costs 107	Schreibkosten, Bürokosten
closing balance sheet 16	Schlussbilanz
closing entry 17	Abschlussbuchung
Commercial Code 10	Handelsgesetzbuch
commitment 120	Bindung
common stock 31	Stammaktie
common stockholder 31	Stammaktionär
company's annual report 42	Geschäftsbericht eines Unternehmens
comparison of budget with actual figures 93	Soll-Ist-Vergleich
compasses 118	Zirkel
compensation 101	Schadenersatz, Entschädigung
compete 118	im Wettbewerb stehen, konkurrieren, sich messen
competition 101	Konkurrenz, Wettbewerb
competitive 101	wettbewerbsfähig, konkurrenzfähig
competitor 43	Mitbewerber, Konkurrent
comply with the law 56	sich an die Gesetze halten
consider 105	betrachten, erwägen, berücksichtigen
consistency concept 11	Bewertungsstetigkeit
consistent with 114	in Übereinstimmung mit, im Einklang mit
consolidated balance sheet 33	Konzernbilanz, konsolidierte Bilanz
consolidated financial statements 33	Konzernabschluss
consolidated income statement 33	Konzern-Gewinn- und Verlustrechnung
consolidated profit and loss account 33	Konzern-Gewinn- und Verlustrechnung
consolidated retained earnings 33	Konzerngewinn

consulting 54	Beratung
contents 12	Inhalt
contribution margin 76, 84	Deckungsbeitrag
contribution margin per unit 76	Deckungsbeitrag pro Stück
contribution margin steps 95	Deckungsbeitragsstufen
corporation 12, 31, 53	Kapitalgesellschaft
cost 11	Kosten
cost 66	kalkulieren, kosten
cost accounting 51	Kostenrechnung
cost center 52	Kostenstelle
cost center accounting 52, 55	Kostenstellenrechnung
cost distribution sheet 52, 55	Betriebsabrechnungsbogen
cost driver 74	Kostentreiber
cost element accounting 52	Kostenartenrechnung
cost elements 52	Kostenarten
cost object 65	Kostenträger
cost of goods manufactured 53	Herstellungskosten
cost of production 65	Herstellkosten
cost of sales 23	Anschaffungs- und Herstellkosten der verkauften Ware, Wareneinsatz, Selbstkosten, Umsatzkosten
cost of sales accounting method 53	Umsatzkostenverfahren
cost of sales method 73	Umsatzkostenverfahren
cost per unit 51	Stückkosten
cost price 65	Selbstkosten
cost type accounting 52	Kostenartenrechnung
cost types 52	Kostenarten
costing 53	Kostenermittlung
costs 25	Kosten
credit 16	Haben
credit an account 17	eine Habenbuchung vornehmen
credit balance 17	Habensaldo
creditor 10	Gläubiger
currency 100	Währung
current assets 13	Umlaufvermögen
current liabilities 13	kurzfristige Verbindlichkeiten

current market value 53	Tageswert
current ratio 42	Liquiditätskennzahl (Umlaufvermögen : kurzfristige Verbindlichkeiten)
curvilinear 74	krummlinig, gekrümmt
customer's reference number 102	Kundennummer
data privacy 102	Datenschutz
data protection 102	Datenschutz
date stamp 118	Datumsstempel
debit 100	Abbuchung
debit 100	abbuchen, belasten
debit 16	Soll
debit an account 16	eine Sollbuchung vornehmen
debit balance 17	Sollsaldo
debt capital 32	Fremdkapital (langfristig)
debt ratio 43	Verschuldungsgrad
declare 100	versteuern
declining-balance method of depreciation 53	degressive Abschreibung
decrease 16	abnehmen, sich vermindern
default 100	Zahlungsverzug
default 100	in Zahlungsverzug geraten
defer 13, 91	hinausschieben, verschieben, verzögern
deferred income 13	Rechnungsabgrenzungsposten der Passivseite
deferred income tax 29	Einkommensteuerverbindlichkeit, Steuerstundung
deferred payment 100	Stundung der Zahlung
deliberately 90	vorsätzlich, absichtlich
denominator 42	Nenner
deplete 29	Bodenschätze abschreiben
depletion 29	Abschreibung von Bodenschätzen (Substanzverzehr)
depletion expense 29	Aufwand für Substanzverzehr, z. B. Abbau von Bodenschätzen
depreciable cost 27	abschreibbare Kosten eines Gutes des Anlagevermögens
depreciate 21, 29	abschreiben
depreciation 11, 13, 21, 27, 51, 99	Abschreibung

depreciation expense 27	Abschreibungsaufwand
depreciation for tax purposes 53	steuerliche Abschreibungen
depreciation method 27	Abschreibungsmethode
depreciation rate 28	Abschreibungsrate, Prozentsatz der Abschreibung
derive 12	ableiten
deterioration 106	Verschlechterung, (Wert-)Minderung, Verderb
digit 10	Ziffer, Dezimalstelle
direct allocation method 57	Anbauverfahren
direct costing 82	Teilkostenrechnung
direct costs 51, 82	Einzelkosten, direkte Kosten
direct debit 103	Abbuchungs-, Einzugsverfahren, Lastschrift
direct debit authorization 103	Einzugsermächtigung
direct material 51	Fertigungsmaterial, Produktionsmaterial
direct method 57	Anbauverfahren
disclose 13	bekannt machen, mitteilen
disclosure 12	Offenlegung, Bekanntmachung
discount rate 120	Abzinsungssatz
discounted payback method 130	dynamische Amortisationsrechnung
dismiss 99	entlassen
dismissal 99	Entlassung
dispose of 91	beseitigen, verkaufen, loswerden
distort 90	verzerren, verdrehen
dividend 32	Dividende
divorced 99	geschieden
domestic 101	inländisch
double-entry system 16	System der doppelten Buchführung
downward demand spiral 94	abwärtsgerichtete Nachfragespirale, spiralförmig abnehmende Nachfrage
draw up 10	aufstellen
drawing pin 118	Heftzwecke
due date 32	Fälligkeitstag
duration 132	Dauer
earnings 10	Ertrag, Einkommen
earnings per share 45	Ergebnis pro Aktie
earnings reserves 14	Gewinnrücklage

economic order quantity (EOQ) 105	optimale Bestellmenge
economics 99	Wirtschaftslehre, Volkswirtschaftslehre, Wirtschaftswissenschaft
economy of scale 102	Kostendegression
elaborate 114	sorgfältig ausgearbeitet
elapse 112, 120	vergehen, verfließen, verstreichen
enter 16	buchen
entity 10	Einheit, Funktionseinheit, juristische Person
entrepreneur 101	Unternehmer
entry 16	Buchung
envelope 118	(Brief-)Umschlag
equal 17	gleichen, gleich sein, ergeben
equity 10	Eigenkapital
equity and liabilities 10	Passivseite der Bilanz
eraser (A. E.) 118	Radiergummi
European Central Bank (ECB) 100	Europäische Zentralbank
examination 42	Prüfung
excessive 97	übermäßig
expenditure 13	Ausgabe
expense 11	Aufwand
expenses 25	Kosten, Aufwendungen
expire under statute of limitations 104	verjähren
expiry date 101	Verfallsdatum
explanatory 12	erklärend, erläuternd
extent 12	Umfang
file 118	Akte
filing cabinet 118	Aktenschrank
financial position 12	Finanzlage
financial statements 10	Jahresabschluss
fiscal policy (Keynesianism) 102	Fiskalpolitik, Keynesianismus
fiscal year 20	Abrechnungsjahr, Geschäftsjahr
fixed assets 13	Anlagevermögen
fixed costs 51	Fixkosten, fixe Kosten

flexible budget 92	Sollkosten
float a company 101	ein Unternehmen an die Börse bringen
flotation 101	Börsengang
fluctuate 101	schwanken
fluctuation 101	Schwankung
folder 118	Schnellhefter, Aktendeckel, Mappe
forge 100	fälschen, nachmachen
forgery 103	Banknotenfälschung
fountain pen 118	Füller, Füllfederhalter
free of charge 101	kostenlos
free-market ideology 102	Idee der freien Markwirtschaft
full costing 82	Vollkostenrechnung
fund 10	Vorrat, Geldmittel
funds 120	Mittel
gain on sale 29	Veräußerungsgewinn
GDP (gross domestic product) 101	Bruttoinlandsprodukt (BIP)
General Business Conditions 99	allgemeine Geschäftsbedingungen
general manager 53	Geschäftsführer
general partner 31	Komplementär, Vollhafter
general partnership 31, 52	offene Handelsgesellschaft, OHG
Generell Accepted Accounting Principles (US-GAAP) 10, 35	Grundsätze ordnungsgemäßer Buchführung (GoB)
German bank's credit reference agency 102	SCHUFA
give notice 99	kündigen
glue 118	Klebstoff
glut 101	Übermaß, Überangebot
GNP (gross national product) 101	Bruttosozialprodukt (BSP)
going concern concept 11	Unternehmensfortführung
goodwill 13	Geschäfts- oder Firmenwert
govern 103	regeln
grace period 101	Zahlungsfrist
grant 101	gewähren, bewilligen
gross 100	brutto
gross domestic product (GDP) 101	Bruttoinlandsprodukt (BIP)

gross (profit) margin 45, 85	Bruttogewinn, Rohertrag, Bruttogewinnspanne
gross national product (GNP) 101	Bruttosozialprodukt (BSP)
group 33	Konzern
guarantee 102	Bürgschaft
guarantor 102	Bürge, Garant
guillotine 118	Papierschneidemaschine
handling charge 100	Bearbeitungsgebühr
heading 12	Posten
highly leveraged 44	stark fremdkapitalfinanziert
historical cost principle 11	Anschaffungskostenprinzip
holding costs 106	Lager(-haltungs)kosten
hospitality 54	Bewirtung, Gastlichkeit
idle time 112	Stillstandszeit, Leerlaufzeit, Wartezeit
impact 79	Einfluss, (Aus-)Wirkung
imparity principle 11	Imparitätsprinzip
impute 53	zuschreiben, beimessen, anrechnen
imputed costs 54	kalkulatorische Kosten
imputed depreciation 53	kalkulatorische Abschreibung
imputed entrepreneurial salary 52	kalkulatorischer Unternehmerlohn
imputed interest 54	kalkulatorische Zinsen
imputed risk costs 54	kalkulatorische Wagniskosten
in advance 103	im Voraus
in compliance with 12	in Übereinstimmung mit
incentive wage 52	Leistungslohn
include 82	enthalten, einbeziehen
income 11	Ertrag, Einkommen
income statement 17, 84	Gewinn- und Verlustrechnung, Ergebnisrechnung
income summary 17	Gewinn- und Verlustkonto
increase 16	zunehmen, sich vergrößern, wachsen
increment 106	Wachstum, Zuwachs, Zunahme
incur 25, 82	auf sich laden, auf sich nehmen
indirect costs 51	Gemeinkosten
initial public offering (IPO) 101	Börsengang
ink-pad 118	Stempelkissen
installment 100	Rate

insurance premium 51	Versicherungsbeitrag
intangible 13	unberührbar, immateriell
intangible assets 102	immaterielle(-s) Vermögen(-swerte)
intercompany transactions 33	Konzerngeschäftsvorfälle, Geschäfte zwischen verbundenen Unternehmen
interest rate 102	Zinssatz
internal 51	intern
internal cost allocation 56	innerbetriebliche Leistungsverrechnung
internal rate of return 123	interner Zinssatz
internal rate of return method 123	interne Zinssatz Methode
Internal Revenue Service (IRS) 29	Finanzbehörde (USA)
internal services 56	innerbetriebliche Leistungen
internal transfer price 56	innerbetrieblicher Verrechnungspreis
intracompany 56	innerbetrieblich
intracompany services 56	innerbetriebliche Leistungen
intracompany services charging 56	innerbetriebliche Leistungsverrechnung
inventories 13	Vorräte
inventory method 53	Inventurmethode
inventory turnover ratio 43	Lagerumschlagshäufigkeit
investment 38, 120	Investition, Geldanlage, Kapitalanlage
IPO (initial public offering) 101	Börsengang
IRR method 123	interne Zinssatz Methode
irrespective of 107	unabhängig von
issuance 32	Ausgabe
issue 104	ausgeben, emittieren
issue of material 55	Materialausgabe
issuer 32	Aussteller, Ausgeber
joint 66	gemeinschaftlich
joint account 99	Gemeinschaftskonto
joint product 66	Kuppelprodukt
joint production process 66	Kuppelproduktion
journal 18	Grundbuch
journal entry 18	Grundbucheintragung
land-charge 102	Grundschuld

launch something onto the market 101	etwas auf den Markt bringen
lead time 112	Lieferzeit
lease 54	Pacht
ledger 18	Hauptbuch
ledger sheet 19	Kontenblatt
lessee 27	Leasingnehmer
lessor 27	Leasinggeber
liability 10	Verbindlichkeit
liability and equity accounts 16	passive Bestandskonten
limited (liability) company 53	Gesellschaft mit beschränkter Haftung, GmbH
limited partner 31	Kommanditist, Teilhafter
limited partnership 31, 52	Kommanditgesellschaft, KG
line of business 103, 118	Branche
linear programming 95	lineare Programmierung
liquidation 10	Liquidation, Liquidierung
liquidity 35, 42	Liquidität, Zahlungsfähigkeit
liquidity-related contribution 96	liquiditätswirksamer Deckungsbeitrag
location factor 104	Standortfaktor
long-term liabilities 13	langfristige Verbindlichkeiten
loss on sale 29	Veräußerungsverlust
lump sum 86	Pauschalbetrag
magnetic strip 100	Magnetstreifen
mail order business 101	Versandunternehmen
main product 66	Hauptprodukt
maintenance 91	Wartung, Instandhaltung
management report 12	Lagebericht
managing partner 53	geschäftsführender Gesellschafter
manufacturing assets 53	Produktionsmittel
manufacturing cost 82	Herstellkosten
manufacturing cost center 55	Fertigungskostenstelle
manufacturing overhead rate 65	Fertigungsgemeinkostenzuschlag
manufacturing supplies 53	Hilfs- und Betriebsstoffe
marginal costing 82	Teilkostenrechnung
marginal costs 75, 82	Grenzkosten

marginal revenue 75	Grenzerlös
matching principle 11	Periodenabgrenzung
material cost overhead rate 65	Materialgemeinkostenzuschlag
material costs 53	Materialkosten
material handling charge 65	Materialgemeinkostenzuschlag
maximum stock 112	Höchstbestand
means of payment 103	Zahlungsmittel
measurable 10	messbar
medium-sized 12	mittelgroß
merchandise 17	Handelswaren
method of payment 103	Zahlungsweise
modified rate of return 127	kritischer Sollzinssatz
monetary policy (Friedman) 102	Geldpolitik, Monetarismus
money laundering 102	Geldwäsche
monopoly 74	Monopol
net 100	netto
net income for the year 14	Jahresüberschuss
net loss for the year 14	Jahresfehlbetrag
net present value 121	Kapitalwert
net present value method 121	Kapitalwertmethode
note 100	Geldschein
notes (to the financial statements) 12	Anhang (zum Jahresabschluss)
notice 99	Kündigung
NPV method 121	Kapitalwertmethode
numerator 42	Zähler
obsolescence 106	Veralterung
obsolete 27, 43	veraltet, altmodisch
offsetting prohibited 11	Saldierungsverbot, Verrechnungsverbot
omit 10	weglassen
opening balance 16	Anfangsbestand
opening balance sheet 16	Eröffnungsbilanz
operating costs 101	Betriebskosten
operating department 56	Fachabteilung
operating income 84	Betriebsgewinn

operating result 72	Betriebsergebnis
operating supplies 53	Betriebsstoffe
opportunity costs 54	Opportunitätskosten
oral 99	mündlich
order 59	Ordnung, Anordnung, Reihenfolge, Folge
ordering costs 106	Bestellkosten
ordiance 12	Verordnung
original entry 18	Grundbucheintragung
outlay 120	(Geld-)Ausgabe
output 51	Leistung, Ertrag, Ausstoß, Produktionsmenge
outside services 54	Fremdleistungen
outstanding 99	hervorragend
outweigh 74	übertreffen
overdraft 99	Kontoüberziehung, Überziehungskredit
overdraft facility 99	Dispositionskredit
overdraw 99	überziehen (Konto)
overhead costs 25	Gemeinkosten
overhead expenses 25	Gemeinkosten
overhead percentage cost calculation 65	Zuschlagskalkulation
overhead rate 65	Gemeinkostensatz (als Zuschlagssatz)
overheads 25, 51, 85	Gemeinkosten, indirekte Kosten
overtime payment 52	Überstundenvergütung
overvalued 91	überbewertet
own use 57	Eigenverbrauch
paid-in capital 10	eingezahltes Kapital, Einlagekapital
pair of compasses 118	Zirkel
pair of scissors 118	Schere
pan-European 99	gesamteuropäisch
paper clip 118	Büroklammer
parent company 33	Muttergesellschaft, Konzernobergesellschaft
partial 59	partiell, teilweise
partner 31	Gesellschafter
partnership 31, 52	Personengesellschaft
patent 13	Patent

pay back 102	zurückzahlen
pay in 103	einzahlen
pay in cash 103	bar bezahlen
pay interest (on) 127	verzinsen
pay off 102	tilgen, zurückzahlen
payback method 129	statische Amortisationsrechnung
payback period 129	Amortisationszeit
payment on open account 100	Zahlung gegen Rechnung (mit offenem Zahlungsziel)
pencil sharpener 118	Bleistiftanspitzer
percentage 28, 100	Prozentsatz
period accounting method 72	Gesamtkostenverfahren
period costing 72	Kostenträgerzeitrechnung
permanent capital 32	Eigenkapital + Fremdkapital (langfristig)
perpetual inventory taking 23	permanente Inventur
personal status 103	Familienstand
personnel costs 52	Personalkosten
physical inventory taking 23	Inventur durch körperliche Bestandsaufnahme
piecework 51, 52	Akkordarbeit
plan 51	Plan
planned costs 92	Plankosten
pledge 100	Pfand
pledge 100	verpfänden
pointer 118	Zeigestock
polypoly 75	Polypol
portfolio 101	Portefeuille, Bestand, Depot
post 18	buchen
posting 18	Buchung
preferred stock 31	Vorzugsaktie
preferred stockholder 31	Vorzugsaktionär
premature 71	vorzeitig
prepaid expenses 13	Rechnungsabgrenzungsposten der Aktivseite
preparation 12	Aufstellung, Vorbereitung
prescribe 12	vorschreiben
present value 121	Barwert, Gegenwartswert

price range 104	Preisspanne
price-earnings ratio 46	Kurs-Gewinn-Verhältnis
prime entry 18	Grundbucheintragung
principal 32	Kapital
principle 10	Grundsatz
principle of prudence 11	Vorsichtsprinzip
principles of preparation 10	Aufstellungsgrundsätze
private limited company 53	Gesellschaft mit beschränkter Haftung, GmbH
probationary period 99	Probezeit
proceed 59	fortsetzen, weitermachen
process cost system 65	Divisions(-stufen)kalkulation
product contribution 96	Produktdeckungsbeitrag
product cost accounting 65	Kostenträgerrechnung
product costing 55, 65	Kostenträgerstückrechnung
product costing per period 72	Kostenträgerzeitrechnung
product costing scheme 51, 65	Kalkulationsschema der Kostenträgerrechnung
product group contribution 96	Produktgruppendeckungsbeitrag
production department 56	Produktionsabteilung
profit 10	Ertrag, Gewinn
profit and loss account 17	Gewinn- und Verlustkonto
profit and loss statement 17	Gewinn- und Verlustrechnung
profit margin 45	Gewinnspanne
profit per unit 65	Stückgewinn
profitability 35, 46	Rentabilität
proprietor 31	Inhaber
protection against dismissal 99	Kündigungsschutz
provision 22	Rückstellung
provision for income taxes 22	Aufwand für Ertragsteuer
prudence concept 11	Vorsichtsprinzip
public (limited) comany 31, 53	Aktiengesellschaft, AG
public stock corporation 53	Aktiengesellschaft, AG
punch 118	Locher
purchase 11	Einkauf, Kauf
purchase movements card 106	Einkaufspendelkarte
purchase stock card 106	Einkaufsstammkarte

purchasing department 106	Einkaufsabteilung
purchasing power 100	Kaufkraft
rank 59	einreihen, einordnen, klassifizieren
rate 51	bewerten, bemessen
rate of return 124	Kapitalverzinsung, Rendite
ratio 42	Verhältnis, Quotient
raw material 53	Rohstoff
raw material warehouse 55	Materiallager
real estate 101	Immobilien
realisation principle 11	Realisationsprinzip
receipt 14	Einnahme
receivable 104	Forderung
receivables 43	Forderungen, Außenstände
reciprocal 56	gegenseitig, wechselseitig
reciprocal allocation method 61	simultane Leistungsverrechnung, Kostenstellenausgleichsverfahren
reciprocate 61	austauschen, wechseln
record 16	aufzeichnen, eintragen, registrieren
recoupment 120	Wiedereinbringung von Verlusten, Ausgaben etc.
rectification 72	Berichtigung
rectify 72	berichtigen, verbessern
redemption 11	Ablösung, Tilgung, Rückzahlung
redemption 37	Rückkauf
register 102	eintragen
regulation 10	Vorschrift
reject 121	ablehnen
relate 51	verbinden, verknüpfen, sich beziehen
reminder 100	Mahnung
render 59	leisten, übergeben, unterbreiten
re-order point 105, 112	Meldebestand
repay 102	tilgen, zurückzahlen
repayment 102	Tilgung, Zurückzahlung
replacement cost 53	Wiederbeschaffungskosten
replenish 105	wieder auffüllen, ergänzen, vervollständigen
report 102	Bericht, Reportage, (Schul-)Zeugnis

requisition 106	Anforderung
resident's registration office 99	Einwohnermeldeamt
residual value 27, 53	Restwert
retain 14	zurückbehalten, einbehalten
retained earnings 10	Bilanzgewinn, einbehaltener Gewinn, Gewinnrücklage
retained earnings brought forward 14	Gewinnvortrag
retained profits 10	Bilanzgewinn, einbehaltener Gewinn, Gewinnrücklage
return on equity (ROE) 44	Eigenkapitalrendite, Eigenkapitalrentabilität
return on investment (ROI) 46	Kapitalverzinsung
rubber (B. E.) 118	Radiergummi
ruler 118	Lineal
safety stock 107, 112	eiserner Bestand, Mindestbestand
sale 17	Verkauf
sales contract 99	Kaufvertrag
sales revenues 23	Umsatzerlöse für Waren
sales structure costs 95	Verkaufsstrukturkosten
scissors 118	Schere
scrap 72	Schrott
seasonal sale 101	Schlussverkauf
securities 13	Wertpapiere
seize 100	pfänden
seizure 100	Pfändung
self-employed 101	selbstständig
sequence 59	Reihenfolge, Anordnung, Folge
sequential allocation method 59	Stufenleiterverfahren, Treppenverfahren
service department 56	Nebenkostenstelle
service life 27, 53	Nutzungsdauer
severance payment 52	Abfindung
share 31, 101	Aktie, Anteil, Geschäftsanteil
shareholder 31	Aktionär, Anteilseigner
shrinkage 23	Schwund, Wertverlust, Verminderung
sift the wheat from the chaff 101	die Spreu vom Weizen trennen

significant 90	bedeutsam
size classifications 12	Größenklassen
social security contributions 52	Sozialversicherungsbeiträge
sole proprietor 31	Einzelkaufmann
sole proprietorship 31, 52	Einzelunternehmen
sole trader 31	Einzelkaufmann
solvency 43	Solvenz, Zahlungsfähigkeit, Fähigkeit zur Bezahlung langfristiger Verbindlichkeiten
sophisticated 114	hoch entwickelt, verfeinert
special direct costs 51, 65	Sondereinzelkosten
special direct costs of production 51	Sondereinzelkosten der Fertigung
special direct costs of sales 51	Sondereinzelkosten des Vertriebs
special direct manufacturing costs 51	Sondereinzelkosten der Fertigung
special direct sales cost 51	Sondereinzelkosten des Vertriebs
specimen signature 99	Unterschriftsprobe
split-off point 66	Trennpunkt der Produktion, Zeitpunkt der getrennten Fertigung
spoil 23	vernichten, zerstören, beschädigen
stable 100	stabil
standard costing 92	Standardkostenrechnung, Plankostenrechnung
standing order 99	Dauerauftrag
staple 118	Heftklammer
stapler 118	Heftmaschine
state 11	darlegen, aussagen, festsetzen
statement of account 100	Kontoauszug
statement printer 100	Kontoauszugsdrucker
statute 102	Satzung
statute of limitation 104	Verjährung
statutory limitation period 104	Verjährungsfrist
steep 75	steil
step cost function 75	abschnittsweise definierte Kostenfunktion, Kostenfunktion in Form einer Treppenfunktion
step-down allocation method 59	Stufenleiterverfahren, Treppenverfahren

stepwise contribution accounting 95	stufenweise Deckungsbeitragsrechnung
stock 31	Aktie
stock 107	Lagerbestand
stock dividend 32	Gratisaktie
stock exchange 104	Börse
stockholder 31	Aktionär, Anteilseigner
stocks 104	Aktien, Lager(-bestand)
storage 54	Lagerung
stores department 106	Lagerabteilung
storing charges 88	Lagerkosten
straight-line depreciation 28, 53	lineare Abschreibung
structure costs 95	Strukturkosten (Fixkosten)
structure costs of the product 95	Produktstrukturkosten, Erzeugnisfixkosten
structure costs of the product group 95	Produktgruppenstrukturkosten, Erzeugnisgruppenfixkosten
subscribed capital 14	gezeichnetes Kapital
subsequent 60	nachfolgend, folgend
subsidiary (company) 33, 99	Tochtergesellschaft, Tochterunternehmen
subsidize 99	subventionieren
subtract 13	abziehen, subtrahieren
sum-of-the-years-digits method of depreciation 53	digitale Abschreibung, arithmetisch-degressive Abschreibung
support department 56	Nebenkostenstelle
surplus 91	Überschuss
survey 99	Untersuchung, Analyse, Überblick
syllable 99	Silbe
T-account 16	T-Konto
tamper-proof 100	fälschungssicher
tangible assets 13, 102	Sachanlagen, Sachanlagevermögen
tax bracket 100	Steuerklasse
terminal rate of return 127	kritischer Sollzinssatz
terminal value 127	(Vermögens-) Endwert
the former 33	der/die/das Erstere, erstere(r, s)
the latter 33	der/die/das Letztere, letztere(r, s)

the small print 99	das Kleingedruckte
tie 105	festlegen (Geld), binden
tie up capital 43	Kapital binden, Kapital festlegen
timber 29	Holzbestand, Baumbestand
time-rate wage 52	Zeitlohn
total 10	Bilanzsumme
trace 66	zurückverfolgen, zurückführen
trademark 13	Schutzmarke, Warenzeichen
transaction 16	Transaktion
transfer price 56	Verrechnungspreis
transparency 118	Folie
treasury stock 31	eigene Aktien
trial period 99	Probezeit
true annual percentage rate 102	effektiver Jahreszins
true APR 102	effektiver Jahreszins
turnover rate 113	Umschlagshäufigkeit
typewriter 118	Schreibmaschine
uncertainty 112	Unsicherheit
unit cost 51	Stückkosten
unit of cost 52	Kostenträger
unit price 65	Stückpreis
unit-of-production depreciation 53	Leistungsabschreibung, stückbezogene Abschreibung
unit-of-production depreciation method 27	Abschreibungsmethode nach Produktionseinheiten
useful life 27, 53	(technische) Lebensdauer, Nutzungsdauer
US-GAAP (Generell Accepted Accounting Principles) 10, 35	GoB (Grundsätze ordnungsgemäßer Buchführung)
utilities 54	Energieversorgungsbetriebe
utilization 93	Verwendung, Anwendung, Inanspruchnahme
valuation provisions 11	Bewertungsvorschriften
value for money 99	Preis-Leistungs-Verhältnis
variable costing 82	Teilkostenrechnung
variable costs 51	variable Kosten
variance 51, 93	Abweichung

variance analysis 93	Abweichungsanalyse
verbal 99	mündlich
vocational school 99	Berufsschule
voluntary employee benefit expenses 52	freiwillige soziale Aufwendungen
voucher 51, 92	Beleg
waste 72	Abfall
wasting asset 29	kurzfristig abnutzbares Wirtschaftsgut
wear and tear 53, 99	Abnutzung, Verschleiß
wear out 27	abnutzen, verbrauchen
weigh up the pros and cons 103	das Für und Wider abwägen
widowed 99	verwitwet
withdraw 18	abheben, entnehmen
withdrawal 18, 100	Abhebung, Entnahme
without notice 99	fristlos
working capital 32	kurzfristiges Betriebskapital (= Umlaufvermögen abzüglich der kurzfristigen Verbindlichkeiten)
write off 21, 29, 53	abschreiben
zero-coupon bond 32	Nullcouponanleihe, abgezinste Anleihe

Alphabetical Vocabulary List (German - English)

abbuchen	debit 100
Abbuchung	debit 100
Abbuchungsverfahren	direct debit 103
ABC-Analyse	ABC classification method 114
Abfall	waste 72
Abfindung	severance payment 52
abgezinste Anleihe	zero-coupon bond 32
abheben	withdraw 18
Abhebung	withdrawal 18, 100
ablehnen	reject 121
ableiten	derive 12
Ablösung	redemption 11
abnehmen	decrease 16
abnutzen	wear out 27
Abnutzung	wear and tear 53, 99
Abrechnungsjahr	fiscal year 20
Abrechnungszeitraum	accounting period 20
Abschlussbuchung	closing entry 17
abschnittsweise definierte Kostenfunktion	step cost function 75
abschreibbare Kosten eines Gutes des Anlagevermögens	depreciable cost 27
abschreiben	depreciate 21, 29, write off 21, 29, 53
Abschreibung	depreciation 11, 13, 21, 27, 51, 99
Abschreibung auf immaterielle Vermögenswerte	amortization 29
Abschreibung von Bodenschätzen (Substanzverzehr)	depletion 29
Abschreibungsaufwand	depreciation expense 27
Abschreibungsmethode	depreciation method 27
Abschreibungsmethode nach Produktionseinheiten	unit-of-production depreciation method 27
Abschreibungsrate	depreciation rate 28
absichtlich	deliberately 90
absorbieren	absorb 91
abwägen	balance 111

abwärtsgerichtete Nachfragespirale	downward demand spiral 94
Abweichung	variance 51, 93
Abweichungsanalyse	variance analysis 93
abziehen	subtract 13
Abzinsungssatz	discount rate 120
AG (Aktiengesellschaft)	public (limited) comany 31, 53, public stock corporation 53
Akkordarbeit	piecework 51, 52
Akte	file 118
Aktendeckel	folder 118
Aktenschrank	filing cabinet 118
Aktie	share 31, 101, stock 31
Aktiengesellschaft (AG)	public (limited) comany 31, 53, public stock corporation 53
Aktionär	shareholder 31, stockholder 31
aktive Bestandskonten	asset accounts 16
Aktivseite der Bilanz	assets 10
allgemeine Geschäftsbedingungen	General Business Conditions 99
altmodisch	obsolete 27, 43
Amortisationszeit	payback period 129
Analyse	survey 99
Anbauverfahren	direct (allocation) method 57
Anfangsbestand	beginning balance 16, opening balance 16
Anforderung	requisition 106
Angleichung	adjustment 36, 85
Anhang (zum Jahresabschluss)	notes (to the financial statements) 12
anhäufen	accumulate 13
Anlagevermögen	fixed assets 13
Anleihe	bond 32
annehmen	assume 11
Annuität	annuity 122
Anordnung	order 59, sequence 59
Anpassung	adjustment 36, 85
anrechnen	impute 53

Anrecht	claim 10
ansammeln	accumulate 13
Anschaffung	acquisition 27
Anschaffungskosten	acquisition costs 27, 53, 120
Anschaffungskostenprinzip	historical cost principle 11
Anschaffungs- und Herstellkosten der verkauften Ware	cost of sales 23
Anspruch	claim 10
Anteil	share 31, 101
Anteilseigner	shareholder 31, stockholder 31
Antragsformular	application form 99
Anwendung	utilization 93
arithmetisch-degressive Abschreibung	sum-of-the-years-digits method of depreciation 53
auf sich laden	incur 25, 82
auf sich nehmen	incur 25, 82
Aufbau	buildup 97
aufgelaufene Abschreibungen	accumulated depreciation 28
aufnehmen	absorb 91
aufstellen	draw up 10
Aufstellung	preparation 12
Aufstellungsgrundsätze	principles of preparation 10
Aufwand	expense 11
Aufwand für Ertragsteuer	provision for income taxes 22
Aufwand für Substanzverzehr, z. B. Abbau von Bodenschätzen	depletion expense 29
aufzeichnen	record 16
Ausbildung(-sverhältnis)	apprenticeship 99
Ausgabe	expenditure 13
Ausgabe	issuance 32
ausgeben	issue 104
Ausgeber	issuer 32
aussagen	state 11
Außenstände	receivables 43
Aussteller	issuer 32

Ausstoß	output 51
austauschen	reciprocate 61
(Aus-)Wirkung	impact 79
Banknotenfälschung	forgery 103
bar bezahlen	pay in cash 103
Barwert	present value 121
Baumbestand	timber 29
Bearbeitungsgebühr	handling charge 100
bedeutsam	significant 90
beimessen	impute 53
bekannt machen	disclose 13
Bekanntmachung	disclosure 12
belasten	debit 100
Beleg	voucher 51, 92
bemessen	rate 51
Benchmarking	benchmarking 118
Beratung	consulting 54
berechnen	calculate 23
Bericht	report 102
berichtigen	rectify 72
Berichtigung	adjustment 36, 85, rectification 72
berücksichtigen	consider 105
Berufsschule	vocational school 99
beschädigen	spoil 23
beseitigen	dispose of 91
Bestand	portfolio 101
Bestellkosten	ordering costs 106
bestimmen	assign 24
betrachten	consider 105
Betriebsabrechnungsbogen	cost distribution sheet 52, 55
Betriebsergebnis	operating result 72
Betriebsgewinn	operating income 84
Betriebskosten	operating costs 101
Betriebsprüfer	auditor 42
Betriebsstoffe	operating supplies 53

Betriebswirtschaftslehre	business administration 3
bewerten	rate 51
Bewertungsstetigkeit	consistency concept 11
Bewertungsvorschriften	valuation provisions 11
bewilligen	grant 101
Bewirtung	hospitality 54
Bezugsgröße	activity unit 55, 65, 99
Bezugswert	benchmark 118
Bilanz	balance sheet 10
Bilanzgewinn	retained earnings 10, retained profits 10
Bilanzidentität	balance sheet continuity 11
Bilanzkontinuität	balance sheet continuity 11
Bilanzstichtag	balance sheet date 13
Bilanzsumme	balance sheet total 10, total 10
binden	tie 105
Bindung	commitment 120
Bleistiftanspitzer	pencil sharpener 118
Bodenschätze abschreiben	deplete 29
Bond	bond 32
Börse	stock exchange 104
Börsengang	initial public offering (IPO) 101, flotation 101
Branche	line of business 103, 118
(Brief-)Umschlag	envelope 118
brutto	gross 100
Bruttogewinn	gross (profit) margin 45, 85
Bruttogewinnspanne	gross (profit) margin 45, 85
Bruttoinlandsprodukt (BIP)	gross domestic product (GDP) 101
Bruttosozialprodukt (BSP)	gross national product (GNP) 101
buchen	book 16, enter 16, post 18
Buchführung	bookkeeping 10
buchmäßige Abschreibung	balance sheet depreciation 53
Buchprüfung	audit 12
Buchung	entry 16, 18, posting 18

Buchwert	book value 28
Bürge	guarantor 102
Bürgschaft	guarantee 102
Büroklammer	paper clip 118
Bürokosten	clerical costs 107
Cash Flow	cash flow 35
darlegen	state 11
das Für und Wider abwägen	weigh up the pros and cons 103
das Kleingedruckte	the small print 99
Datenschutz	data privacy 102, data protection 102
Datumsstempel	date stamp 118
Dauer	duration 132
Dauerauftrag	standing order 99
Deckungsbeitrag	contribution margin 76, 84
Deckungsbeitrag pro Stück	contribution margin per unit 76
Deckungsbeitragsstufen	contribution margin steps 95
degressive Abschreibung	declining-balance method of depreciation 53
Depot	portfolio 101
der/die/das Erstere	the former 33
der/die/das Letztere	the latter 33
Dezimalstelle	digit 10
die Spreu vom Weizen trennen	sift the wheat from the chaff 101
digitale Abschreibung	sum-of-the-years-digits method of depreciation 53
direkte Kosten	direct costs 51, 82
Dispositionskredit	overdraft facility 99
Dividende	dividend 32
Divisions(-stufen)kalkulation	process cost system 65
durchschnittliche Lagerdauer	average time of storage 113
durchschnittlicher Lagerbestand	average stock 108
Durchschnittskosten	average cost 51
dynamische Amortisationsrechnung	discounted payback method 130
Eckdaten	basic data 102

effektiver Jahreszins	true annual percentage rate 102, true APR 102
eigene Aktien	treasury stock 31
Eigenkapital	equity 10
Eigenkapital + Fremdkapital (langfristig)	permanent capital 32
Eigenkapitalrendite	return on equity (ROE) 44
Eigenkapitalrentabilität	return on equity (ROE) 44
Eigenverbrauch	own use 57
ein den tatsächlichen Verhältnissen entsprechendes Bild	a true and fair view 12
ein Unternehmen an die Börse bringen	float a company 101
einbehalten	retain 14
einbehaltener Gewinn	retained earnings 10, retained profits 10
einbeziehen	include 82
eine Habenbuchung vornehmen	credit an account 17
eine Sollbuchung vornehmen	debit an account 16
Einfluss	impact 79
eingezahltes Kapital	paid-in capital 10
Einheit	entity 10
Einkauf	purchase 11
Einkaufsabteilung	purchasing department 106
Einkaufspendelkarte	purchase movements card 106
Einkaufsstammkarte	purchase stock card 106
Einkommen	earnings 10, income 11
Einkommensteuerverbindlichkeit	deferred income tax 29
Einlagekapital	paid-in capital 10
Einnahme	receipt 14
einordnen	rank 59
einreihen	rank 59
Einstandskosten	acquisition costs 27, 53, 120
eintragen	record 16, register 102
Einwohnermeldeamt	resident's registration office 99
einzahlen	pay in 103
Einzelkaufmann	sole proprietor 31, sole trader 31

Einzelkosten	direct costs 51, 82
Einzelunternehmen	sole proprietorship 31, 52
Einzugsermächtigung	direct debit authorization 103
Einzugsverfahren	direct debit 103
eiserner Bestand	base stock 107, 112, safety stock 107, 112
emittieren	issue 104
Energieversorgungsbetriebe	utilities 54
Engpass	bottleneck 75
enthalten	include 82
entlassen	dismiss 99
Entlassung	dismissal 99
Entnahme	withdrawal 18, 100
entnehmen	withdraw 18
Entschädigung	compensation 101
ergänzen	replenish 105
ergeben	equal 17
Ergebnis pro Aktie	earnings per share 45
Ergebnisrechnung	income statement 17, 84
erklärend	explanatory 12
erlangen	acquire 10
erläuternd	explanatory 12
Eröffnungsbilanz	opening balance sheet 16
erstere(r, s)	the former 33
Ertrag	earnings 10, profit 10, income 11, output 51
erwägen	consider 105
Erwerb	acquisition 27
erwerben	acquire 10
Erzeugnisfixkosten	structure costs of the product 95
Erzeugnisgruppenfixkosten	structure costs of the product group 95
etwas auf den Markt bringen	launch something onto the market 101
Europäische Zentralbank	European Central Bank (ECB) 100
Fachabteilung	operating department 56

Fähigkeit	ability 42
Fähigkeit zur Bezahlung langfristiger Verbindlichkeiten	solvency 43
Fälligkeitstag	due date 32
fälschen	forge 100
fälschungssicher	tamper-proof 100
Familienstand	personal status 103
Fertigungsgemeinkostenzuschlag	manufacturing overhead rate 65
Fertigungskostenstelle	manufacturing cost center 55
Fertigungsmaterial	direct material 51
festlegen	assign 24
festlegen (Geld)	tie 105
festsetzen	state 11, assign 24
Finanzbehörde (USA)	Internal Revenue Service (IRS) 29
Finanzlage	financial position 12
Fiskalpolitik	fiscal policy (Keynesianism) 102
fixe Kosten	fixed costs 51
Fixkosten	fixed costs 51
Folge	order 59, sequence 59
folgend	subsequent 60
Folie	transparency 118
Forderung	claim 10, receivable 104
Forderungen	accounts receivable 13, receivables 43
fortsetzen	proceed 59
freiwillige soziale Aufwendungen	voluntary employee benefit expenses 52
Fremdkapital (langfristig)	debt capital 32
Fremdleistungen	outside services 54
fristlos	without notice 99
Füller, Füllfederhalter	fountain pen 118
Funktionseinheit	entity 10
Garant	guarantor 102
Gastlichkeit	hospitality 54
Gastronomie	catering 99

gegenseitig	reciprocal 56
Gegenwartswert	present value 121
gekrümmt	curvilinear 74
Geldanlage	investment 38, 120
(Geld-)Ausgabe	outlay 120
Geldeingang	cash receipt 20
Geldmittel	fund 10
Geldpolitik	monetary policy (Friedman) 102
Geldschein	note 100
Geldwäsche	money laundering 102
Gemeinkosten	indirect costs 51, overhead costs 25, overhead expenses 25, overheads 25, 51, 85
Gemeinkostensatz	burden rate 65
Gemeinkostensatz (als Zuschlagssatz)	overhead rate 65
Gemeinkostenumlage	apportionment of indirect cost 65
Gemeinkostenverrechnungssatz	allocation rate 65
gemeinschaftlich	joint 66
Gemeinschaftskonto	joint account 99
genau	accurate 61
gesamteuropäisch	pan-European 99
Gesamtkostenverfahren	period accounting method 72
Geschäfte zwischen verbundenen Unternehmen	intercompany transactions 33
Geschäftsanteil	share 31, 101
Geschäfts- oder Firmenwert	goodwill 13
Geschäftsbericht	annual report 12
Geschäftsbericht eines Unternehmens	company's annual report 42
geschäftsführender Gesellschafter	managing partner 53
Geschäftsführer	general manager 53
Geschäftsjahr	fiscal year 20
geschieden	divorced 99
Gesellschaft mit beschränkter Haftung (GmbH)	limited (liability) company 53, private limited company 53
Gesellschafter	partner 31
Gesellschaftssatzung	articles of association 104

Gesellschaftsvertrag	articles of association 104
gewähren	grant 101
Gewinn	profit 10
Gewinn- und Verlustkonto	income summary 17, profit and loss account 17
Gewinn- und Verlustrechnung	income statement 17, 84, profit and loss statement 17
Gewinnrücklage	retained earnings 10, retained profits 10, earnings reserves 14
Gewinnschwelle	break-even point 75
Gewinnspanne	profit margin 45
Gewinnvortrag	retained earnings brought forward 14
gezeichnetes Kapital	subscribed capital 14
Gläubiger	creditor 10
gleich sein	equal 17
gleichen	equal 17
GmbH (Gesellschaft mit beschränkter Haftung)	limited (liability) company 53, private limited company 53
GoB (Grundsätze ordnungsgemäßer Buchführung)	US-GAAP (Generell Accepted Accounting Principles) 10, 35
Gratisaktie	stock dividend 32
Grenzerlös	marginal revenue 75
Grenzkosten	marginal costs 75, 82
Größenklassen	size classifications 12
Grundbuch	book of original 18, journal 18
Grundbucheintragung	journal entry 18, original entry 18, prime entry 18
Grundsatz	principle 10
Grundsätze ordnungsgemäßer Buchführung (GoB)	Generell Accepted Accounting Principles (US-GAAP) 10, 35
Grundschuld	land-charge 102
Haben	credit 16
Habensaldo	credit balance 17
Handelsgesetzbuch	Commercial Code 10
Handelswaren	merchandise 17
Hauptbuch	ledger 18

Hauptprodukt	main product 66
Heftklammer	staple 118
Heftmaschine	stapler 118
Heftzwecke	drawing pin 118
Herstellkosten	cost of production 65, manufacturing cost 82
Herstellungskosten	cost of goods manufactured 53
hervorragend	outstanding 99
Hilfs- und Betriebsstoffe	manufacturing supplies 53
hinausschieben	defer 13, 91
hoch entwickelt	sophisticated 114
Höchstbestand	maximum stock 112
Holzbestand	timber 29
Idee der freien Markwirtschaft	free-market ideology 102
im Einklang mit	consistent with 114
im Haushaltsplan vorsehen	budget 83
im Voraus	in advance 103
im Wettbewerb stehen	compete 118
immateriell	intangible 13
immaterielle(-s) Vermögen(-swerte)	intangible assets 102
Immobilien	real estate 101
Imparitätsprinzip	imparity principle 11
in den roten Zahlen sein	be in the red 100
in Übereinstimmung mit	in compliance with 12, consistent with 114
in Zahlungsverzug geraten	default 100
Inanspruchnahme	utilization 93
indirekte Kosten	overheads 25, 51, 85
Inhaber	proprietor 31
Inhalt	contents 12
inländisch	domestic 101
innerbetrieblich	intracompany 56
innerbetriebliche Leistungen	internal services 56, intracompany services 56
innerbetriebliche Leistungsverrechnung	internal cost allocation 56, intracompany services charging 56

innerbetrieblicher Verrechnungspreis	internal transfer price 56
Instandhaltung	maintenance 91
intern	internal 51
interne Zinssatz Methode	internal rate of return method 123, IRR method 123
interner Zinssatz	internal rate of return 123
Inventur durch körperliche Bestandsaufnahme	physical inventory taking 23
Inventurmethode	inventory method 53
Investition	investment 38, 120
Istkosten	actual costs 92
Istleistung	actual activity 93
Jahresabschluss	financial statements 10, annual financial statements 33
Jahresfehlbetrag	net loss for the year 14
Jahresüberschuss	net income for the year 14
Jahreszins	annual percentage rate (APR) 102
(jährlich) identische Beträge	annuity 122
juristische Person	entity 10
Kalkulationsschema der Kostenträgerrechnung	product costing scheme 51, 65
kalkulatorische Abschreibung	imputed depreciation 53
kalkulatorische Kosten	imputed costs 54
kalkulatorische Wagniskosten	imputed risk costs 54
kalkulatorische Zinsen	imputed interest 54
kalkulatorischer Unternehmerlohn	imputed entrepreneurial salary 52
kalkulieren	calculate 23, cost 66
Kapazität	capacity 76
Kapital	principal 32
Kapital binden	tie up capital 43
Kapital festlegen	tie up capital 43
Kapitalanlage	investment 38, 120
Kapitalfluss	cash flow 35
Kapitalflussrechnung	cash flow statement 35
Kapitalgesellschaft	corporation 12, 31, 53
Kapitalrücklage	capital reserves 14
Kapitalumschlag	capital turnover 47

Kapitalverzinsung	return on investment (ROI) 46, rate of return 124
Kapitalwert	net present value 121
Kapitalwertmethode	net present value method 121, NPV method 121
Kasseneinnahme	cash receipt 20
Kauf	purchase 11
Kaufkraft	purchasing power 100
Kaufvertrag	sales contract 99
Keynesianismus	Keynesianism (fiscal policy) 102
KG (Kommanditgesellschaft)	limited partnership 31, 52
klassifizieren	rank 59
Klebeband	adhesive tape 118
Klebstoff	glue 118
(das) Kleingedruckte	the small print 99
Kohlepapier	carbon paper 118
Kommanditgesellschaft (KG)	limited partnership 31, 52
Kommanditist	limited partner 31
Komplementär	general partner 31
Konkurrent	competitor 43
Konkurrenz	competition 101
konkurrenzfähig	competitive 101
konkurrieren	compete 118
konsolidierte Bilanz	consolidated balance sheet 33
Kontenblatt	ledger sheet 19
Konto	account 99
Kontoauszug	bank statement 100, statement of account 100
Kontoauszugsdrucker	statement printer 100
Kontoinhaber	account holder 99
Kontostand	account balance 100
Kontoüberziehung	overdraft 99
Konzern	group 33
Konzernabschluss	consolidated financial statements 33
Konzernbilanz	consolidated balance sheet 33

Konzerngeschäftsvorfälle	intercompany transactions 33
Konzerngewinn	consolidated retained earnings 33
Konzern-Gewinn- und Verlustrechnung	consolidated income statement 33, consolidated profit and loss account 33
Konzernobergesellschaft	parent company 33
Kosten	cost 11, costs 25, expenses 25, charges 88
kosten	cost 66
Kostenarten	cost elements 52, cost types 52
Kostenartenrechnung	cost element accounting 52, cost type accounting 52
Kostendegression	economy of scale 102
Kostenermittlung	costing 53
Kostenfunktion in Form einer Treppenfunktion	step cost function 75
kostenlos	free of charge 101
Kostenrechnung	cost accounting 51
Kostenstelle	cost center 52
Kostenstellenausgleichsverfahren	reciprocal allocation method 61
Kostenstellenrechnung	cost center accounting 52, 55
Kostenträger	unit of cost 52, cost object 65
Kostenträgerrechnung	product cost accounting 65
Kostenträgerstückrechnung	product costing 55, 65
Kostenträgerzeitrechnung	period costing 72, product costing per period 72
Kostentreiber	cost driver 74
kritischer Sollzinssatz	modified rate of return 127, terminal rate of return 127
krummlinig	curvilinear 74
Kundennummer	customer´s reference number 102
kündigen	give notice 99
Kündigung	notice 99
Kündigungsschutz	protection against dismissal 99
Kuppelprodukt	joint product 66
Kuppelproduktion	joint production process 66
Kurs-Gewinn-Verhältnis	price-earnings ratio 46

kurzfristig abnutzbares Wirtschaftsgut	wasting asset 29
kurzfristige Verbindlichkeiten	current liabilities 13
kurzfristiges Betriebskapital (= Umlaufvermögen abzüglich der kurzfristigen Verbindlichkeiten)	working capital 32
Ladung	batch 111
Lagebericht	management report 12
Lager(-bestand)	stocks 104
Lagerabteilung	stores department 106
Lagerbestand	stock 107
Lagerbestandskarte	bin card 105
Lagerfachkarte	bin card 105
Lager(-haltungs)kosten	holding costs 106
Lagerkosten	storing charges 88
Lagerumschlagshäufigkeit	inventory turnover ratio 43
Lagerung	storage 54
langfristige Verbindlichkeiten	long-term liabilities 13
Lastschrift	direct debit 103
Leasing	capital lease 27
Leasinggeber	lessor 27
Leasingnehmer	lessee 27
Lebensdauer (technisch)	useful life 27, 53
Leerlaufzeit	idle time 112
Lehre	apprenticeship 99
leisten	render 59
Leistung	output 51
Leistungsabschreibung	unit-of-production depreciation 53
Leistungslohn	incentive wage 52
Leistungsvergleich	benchmarking 118
letztere(r, s)	the latter 33
Lieferzeit	lead time 112
Lineal	ruler 118
lineare Abschreibung	straight-line depreciation 28, 53
lineare Programmierung	linear programming 95
Liquidation	liquidation 10
Liquidierung	liquidation 10

Liquidität	liquidity 35, 42
Liquiditätskennzahl (Umlaufvermögen : kurzfristige Verbindlichkeiten)	current ratio 42
liquiditätswirksamer Deckungsbeitrag	liquidity-related contribution 96
Locher	punch 118
loswerden	dispose of 91
Magnetstreifen	magnetic strip 100
Mahnung	reminder 100
Mappe	folder 118
Maßstab	benchmark 118
Materialausgabe	issue of material 55
Materialgemeinkostenzuschlag	material cost overhead rate 65, material handling charge 65
Materialkosten	material costs 53
Materiallager	raw material warehouse 55
Meldebestand	re-order point 105, 112
messbar	measurable 10
Minderung	deterioration 106
Mindestbestand	base stock 107, 112, safety stock 107, 112
Mitbewerber	competitor 43
mitteilen	disclose 13
Mittel	funds 120
mittelgroß	medium-sized 12
Monetarismus	monetary policy (Friedman) 102
Monopol	monopoly 74
mündlich	oral 99, verbal 99
Muttergesellschaft	parent company 33
nachfolgend	subsequent 60
nachmachen	forge 100
Nebenkostenstelle	service department 56, support department 56
Nebenprodukt	by-product 66
Nenner	denominator 42
netto	net 100
Nullcouponanleihe	zero-coupon bond 32

Nutzungsdauer	service life 27, 53, useful life 27, 53
offene Handelsgesellschaft (OHG)	general partnership 31, 52
Offenlegung	disclosure 12
OHG (offene Handelsgesellschaft)	general partnership 31, 52
Opportunitätskosten	opportunity costs 54
optimale Bestellmenge	economic order quantity (EOQ) 105
Ordnung	order 59
Pacht	lease 54
Papierschneidemaschine	guillotine 118
partiell	partial 59
passive Bestandskonten	liability and equity accounts 16
Passivseite der Bilanz	equity and liabilities 10
Patent	patent 13
Pauschalbetrag	lump sum 86
Periodenabgrenzung	accruals concept 11, matching principle 11
permanente Inventur	perpetual inventory taking 23
Personalkosten	personnel costs 52
Personengesellschaft	partnership 31, 52
Pfand	pledge 100
pfänden	seize 100
Pfändung	seizure 100
Plan	plan 51
planen	budget 83
Plankosten	planned costs 92
Plankostenrechnung	standard costing 92
Polypol	polypoly 75
Portefeuille	portfolio 101
Posten	heading 12
Preis-Leistungs-Verhältnis	value for money 99
Preisspanne	price range 104
Probezeit	probationary period 99, trial period 99
Produktdeckungsbeitrag	product contribution 96

Produktgruppendeckungsbeitrag	product group contribution 96
Produktgruppenstrukturkosten	structure costs of the product group 95
Produktionsabteilung	production department 56
Produktionsmaterial	direct material 51
Produktionsmenge	output 51
Produktionsmittel	manufacturing assets 53
Produktstrukturkosten	structure costs of the product 95
Prozentsatz	percentage 28, 100
Prozentsatz der Abschreibung	depreciation rate 28
Prüfung	examination 42
Prüfungswesen	auditing 42
Quotient	ratio 42
Radiergummi	eraser (A. E.) 118, rubber (B. E.) 118
Rate	installment 100
Realisationsprinzip	realisation principle 11
Rechnungsabgrenzungsposten der Aktivseite	prepaid expenses 13
Rechnungsabgrenzungsposten der Passivseite	deferred income 13
Rechnungsprüfung	auditing 42
Rechnungswesen	accounting 53
Rechnungswesen (Abteilung)	accounts department 106
regeln	govern 103
registrieren	record 16
Reihenfolge	order 59, sequence 59
Rendite	return on investment (ROI) 46, rate of return 124
Rentabilität	profitability 35, 46
Rentabilitätsvergleichsrechnung	accounting rate of return method 131
Rente	annuity 122
Reportage	report 102
Restbestand	balance 16
Restwert	residual value 27, 53
Rohertrag	gross (profit) margin 45, 85
Rohstoff	raw material 53

Rückkauf	redemption 37
Rückstellung	provision 22
Rückstellungen	accruals 13, accrued liabilities 13
Rückzahlung	redemption 11
Sachanlagen, Sachanlagevermögen	tangible assets 13, 102
Saldierungsverbot	offsetting prohibited 11
Saldo	balance 16
Satzung	statute 102
Schadenersatz	compensation 101
Schere	(pair of) scissors 118
schlecht werden	be spoiled 105
Schlussbestand	balance 16
Schlussbilanz	closing balance sheet 16
Schlussverkauf	seasonal sale 101
Schnellhefter	folder 118
Schreibkosten	clerical costs 107
Schreibmaschine	typewriter 118
Schrott	scrap 72
SCHUFA	German bank's credit reference agency 102
Schuldverschreibung	bond 32
(Schul-)Zeugnis	report 102
Schutzmarke	trademark 13
schwanken	fluctuate 101
Schwankung	fluctuation 101
Schwund	shrinkage 23
Selbstkosten	cost of sales 23, cost price 65
selbstständig	self-employed 101
sich an die Gesetze halten	comply with the law 56
sich beziehen	relate 51
sich messen	compete 118
sich vergrößern	increase 16
sich vermindern	decrease 16
Silbe	syllable 99
simultane Leistungsverrechnung	reciprocal allocation method 61

Soll	debit 16
Soll-Ist-Vergleich	comparison of budget with actual figures 93
Sollkosten	flexible budget 92
Sollsaldo	debit balance 17
Solvenz	solvency 43
Sonderabschreibung, die über die normale Abschreibung hinausgeht	accelerated depreciation 28
Sondereinzelkosten	special direct costs 51, 65
Sondereinzelkosten der Fertigung	special direct costs of production 51, special direct manufacturing costs 51
Sondereinzelkosten des Vertriebs	special direct costs of sales 51, special direct sales cost 51
sorgfältig ausgearbeitet	elaborate 114
Sozialversicherungsbeiträge	social security contributions 52
spiralförmig abnehmende Nachfrage	downward demand spiral 94
stabil	stable 100
Stammaktie	common stock 31
Stammaktionär	common stockholder 31
Standardkostenrechnung	standard costing 92
Standortfaktor	location factor 104
Stapel	batch 111
stark fremdkapitalfinanziert	highly leveraged 44
statische Amortisationsrechnung	payback method 129
steil	steep 75
Stempelkissen	ink-pad 118
Steuerklasse	tax bracket 100
steuerliche Abschreibungen	depreciation for tax purposes 53
Steuerstundung	deferred income tax 29
Stillstandszeit	idle time 112
Strukturkosten (Fixkosten)	structure costs 95
stückbezogene Abschreibung	unit-of-production depreciation 53
Stückgewinn	profit per unit 65
Stückkosten	cost per unit 51, unit cost 51
Stückpreis	unit price 65

Stufenleiterverfahren	sequential allocation method 59, step-down allocation method 59
stufenweise Deckungsbeitragsrechnung	stepwise contribution accounting 95
Stundung der Zahlung	deferred payment 100
subtrahieren	subtract 13
subventionieren	subsidize 99
System der doppelten Buchführung	double-entry system 16
Tageswert	current market value 53
Taschenrechner	calculator 118
(technische) Lebensdauer	useful life 27, 53
Teilhafter	limited partner 31
Teilkostenrechnung	direct costing 82, marginal costing 82, variable costing 82
teilweise	partial 59
tilgen	repay 102, pay off 102
Tilgung	redemption 11, repayment 102
Tintenpatrone	cartridge 118
T-Konto	T-account 16
Tochtergesellschaft	subsidiary (company) 33, 99
Tochterunternehmen	subsidiary (company) 33, 99
Transaktion	transaction 16
Trennpunkt der Produktion	split-off point 66
Treppenverfahren	sequential allocation method 59, step-down allocation method 59
Überangebot	glut 101
überbewertet	overvalued 91
Überblick	survey 99
übergeben	render 59
Übermaß	glut 101
übermäßig	excessive 97
Überschuss	surplus 91
Überstundenvergütung	overtime payment 52
übertreffen	outweigh 74
überziehen (Konto)	overdraw 99
Überziehungskredit	overdraft 99

Umfang	extent 12
Umlaufvermögen	current assets 13
Umsatzerlöse für Waren	sales revenues 23
Umsatzkosten	cost of sales 23
Umsatzkostenverfahren	cost of sales accounting method 53, cost of sales method 73
Umschlagshäufigkeit	turnover rate 113
unabhängig von	irrespective of 107
unberührbar	intangible 13
uneinbringliche Forderung	bad debt 21
Unsicherheit	uncertainty 112
unterbreiten	render 59
Unternehmensfortführung	going concern concept 11
Unternehmer	entrepreneur 101
Unterschriftsprobe	specimen signature 99
Untersuchung	survey 99
variable Kosten	variable costs 51
Veralterung	obsolescence 106
veraltet	obsolete 27, 43
Veräußerungsgewinn	gain on sale 29
Veräußerungsverlust	loss on sale 29
verbessern	rectify 72
verbinden	relate 51
Verbindlichkeit	liability 10
Verbindlichkeiten	accounts payable 40
verbrauchen	wear out 27
Verderb	deterioration 106
verdrehen	distort 90
Verfallsdatum	expiry date 101
verfeinert	sophisticated 114
verfließen	elapse 112, 120
vergehen	elapse 112, 120
Verhältnis	ratio 42
verjähren	expire under statute of limitations 104

Verjährung	statute of limitation 104
Verjährungsfrist	statutory limitation period 104
Verkauf	sale 17
verkaufen	dispose of 91
Verkaufsstrukturkosten	sales structure costs 95
verknüpfen	relate 51
Verlustvortrag	accumulated losses brought forward 14
Verminderung	shrinkage 23
(Vermögens-) Endwert	terminal value 127
vernichten	spoil 23
Verordnung	ordiance 12
verpfänden	pledge 100
Verrechnungspreis	transfer price 56
Verrechnungssatz	allocation rate 55
Verrechnungsverbot	offsetting prohibited 11
Versandunternehmen	mail order business 101
verschieben	defer 13, 91
Verschlechterung	deterioration 106
Verschleiß	wear and tear 53, 99
Verschuldungsgrad	debt ratio 43
Versicherungsbeitrag	insurance premium 51
versteigern	auction off 100
versteuern	declare 100
verstreichen	elapse 112, 120
vervollständigen	replenish 105
Verwaltungsstrukturkosten	administration structure costs 96
Verwendung	utilization 93
verwitwet	widowed 99
verzerren	distort 90
verzinsen	pay interest (on) 127
verzögern	defer 13, 91
Volkswirtschaftslehre	economics 99
Vollhafter	general partner 31
Vollkostenrechnung	absorption costing 82, full costing 82

Vorauszahlung	advance payments 20
Vorbereitung	preparation 12
Vorrat	fund 10
Vorräte	inventories 13
vorsätzlich	deliberately 90
vorschreiben	prescribe 12
Vorschrift	regulation 10
Vorschuss	advance 20
Vorsichtsprinzip	principle of prudence 11, prudence concept 11
vorzeitig	premature 71
Vorzugsaktie	preferred stock 31
Vorzugsaktionär	preferred stockholder 31
wachsen	increase 16
Wachstum	increment 106
Währung	currency 100
Wareneinsatz	cost of sales 23
Warenzeichen	trademark 13
Wartezeit	idle time 112
Wartung	maintenance 91
wechseln	reciprocate 61
wechselseitig	reciprocal 56
weglassen	omit 10
weitermachen	proceed 59
Wertberichtigung auf Forderungen	allowance for doubtful accounts 21
(Wert-)Minderung	deterioration 106
Wertpapiere	securities 13
Wertverlust	shrinkage 23
Wettbewerb	competition 101
wettbewerbsfähig	competitive 101
wieder auffüllen	replenish 105
Wiederbeschaffungskosten	replacement cost 53
Wiedereinbringung von Verlusten, Ausgaben etc.	recoupment 120
wiegen	balance 111
Wirtschaftslehre	economics 99

Wirtschaftsprüfer	auditor 42
Wirtschaftsprüfung	auditing 42
Wirtschaftswissenschaft	economics 99
Zähler	numerator 42
Zahlung gegen Rechnung (mit offenem Zahlungsziel)	payment on open account 100
Zahlungsfähigkeit	liquidity 35, 42, solvency 43
Zahlungsfrist	grace period 101
Zahlungsmittel	means of payment 103
Zahlungsverzug	default 100
Zahlungsweise	method of payment 103
Zeigestock	pointer 118
Zeitlohn	time-rate wage 52
Zeitpunkt der getrennten Fertigung	split-off point 66
zerstören	spoil 23
Zeugnis	report 102
Ziffer	digit 10
Zinssatz	interest rate 102
Zirkel	(pair of) compasses 118
Zunahme	increment 106
zunehmen	increase 16
zur Verfügung	at your disposal 101
zurückbehalten	retain 14
zurückführen	trace 66
zurückverfolgen	trace 66
zurückzahlen	repay 102, pay off 102, pay back 102
Zurückzahlung	repayment 102
Zuschlagskalkulation	overhead percentage cost calculation 65
Zuschlagssatz	allocation rate 55
zuschreiben	impute 53
zuteilen	assign 51, 82
Zuwachs	increment 106
zuweisen	assign 51, 82